Gourmet Vegetarian Cooking

Rose Elliot is one of Britain's most famous writers on vegetarian cookery. She is the author of many best-selling books and her original and imaginative style has made her a favourite among vegetarians and non-vegetarians alike. Her recipes range from creations of subtle sophistication to simple and cheap dishes for the novice cook and those on a tight budget.

Rose Elliot became a cookery writer by accident. She was planning to take a degree in history when she met and married her husband and became involved in cooking, entertaining and bringing up a family. For many years she has tried out all her recipes at home, the very best of which she has included in her books.

ROSE ELLIOT

Gourmet Vegetarian Cooking

FONTANA/Collins

First published by
William Collins Sons & Co. Ltd 1982
First issued in Fontana 1983
Fourth impression September 1988

Copyright © Rose Elliot 1982

Illustrations by Vana Haggerty

Set in Linotron Times
Printed and bound in Great Britain by
William Collins Sons & Co. Ltd, Glasgow

To Anthony,
with love and thanks

Contents

Introduction

Gourmet cooking means food which truly satisfies the senses: food in which the balance of texture and flavour is exactly right and both looks and tastes delicious. And contrary to what many people believe, such food does not have to contain meat or fish, nor does it necessarily have to be elaborate. Indeed it can be quite simple – an exquisitively ripe peach or perfectly fresh crusty bread are, in my opinion, gourmet foods – and vegetarian dishes have just as much scope and potential for being beautifully presented in tasty meals.

I have collected here some of my favourite recipes which can be used either for your own sheer indulgence or for those special occasions when gourmet food can contribute so much to their success and enjoyment. Occasions when you have friends into your home for a meal, to enjoy good food and drink in a warm and relaxing atmosphere; to linger over the table as the candles burn down and no one wants to move away. Or when you come home after some outdoor activity to delicious cooking smells and share a hearty meal in the kitchen, washed down with plenty of cider or wine. Or the summer meals outside, the special picnics in the country or by the sea, and barbecues in the garden on long, warm evenings.

Food is at the heart of all these occasions but if you're vegetarian, or have vegetarian friends or relations to cook for, these meals can all pose problems. What, for instance, can you eat at a dinner party instead of good meat or fish, or grill at a barbecue, or, that perennial question, have instead of turkey for Christmas dinner?

And whereas meat eaters begin with the advantage of having something substantial such as a turkey or a joint of meat on which to base the meal, vegetarians have to start making their meals from scratch, soaking pulses, chopping vegetables and grinding nuts, with no real tradition to guide them.

On the other hand this lack of convention can be an asset, because it means you are free to experiment and invent new dishes, to try out different flavours and create interesting textures. It's enormously rewarding to surprise and delight people with a mouthwatering meal which doesn't contain any meat.

I say 'surprise' because many people still think that meat or fish are essential to gourmet cookery. Yet with a little imagination you really can produce wonderful vegetarian food for occasions ranging from impromptu meals for two, to grand dinner parties, alfresco summer picnics and formal lunches.

Cooking has become very much easier and more fun now that so many exciting ingredients are readily available. I find much inspiration from looking round markets, specialist food shops and even my local supermarket, and seeing the luscious fruits and vegetables, wonderful cheeses, fragrant herbs and spices, nuts and pulses, all crying out to be tried. And once you start experimenting in the kitchen it is amazing how one discovery leads to another and the ideas keep flowing.

All the recipes in this book, except for one or two classics like cheese fondue, are original ones I have invented for various occasions and tried out successfully on my family and friends. Creamy soups such as golden carrot, apple and chervil, or the velvety green pea soup with cream and mint; some unusual first courses like the stripy pâté, exotic grapefruit rose baskets and the Cheddar cheese and red wine dip, guaranteed to stimulate conversation as well as appetites.

Then there are main dishes for all occasions: shiny golden pies, unusual flans and tartlets which melt in your mouth; vegetable dishes such as hot avocados with wine stuffing, asparagus in hot lemon mayonnaise and stuffed marrow with butter and thyme. Also moist and tasty savoury loaves, such as the white nut meat with capers and the chestnut, sage and red wine loaf; rich-tasting tempting pasta and colourful rice dishes, ideas for accompanying vegetables and salads.

And to end the meal with a flourish, there are delectable puddings ranging from simple vanilla ice cream with hot chestnut and brandy sauce, rose sorbet and peaches in strawberry purée, to the rich and indulgent almond and chocolate flan, cheesecake on a chocolate base or glossy jewelled fruit flan.

Although these dishes are delicious, nearly all of them are quite simple to make. For while I love good food and enjoy making special meals, with three children, one not yet at school, I know very well what it is to have limited time and energy for cooking. So these recipes rely more on imaginative use of good ingredients than elaborate techniques. And, although undeniably more indulgent than some vegetarian dishes, they are still relatively healthy and nutritional, being high in fibre and mostly quite low on sugar and saturated fats. As for the cost, one of the many joys of vegetarian cookery is of course its economy, and while some of the dishes with their more exotic ingredients are naturally more expensive to make, they are easily compensated for by the savings made on meat and fish.

But do you need to justify the expense? Surely one of the greatest satisfactions of life is to cook and serve a really delicious meal, a meal which nourishes the body and cheers the spirit, and may be remembered with pleasure for a long time to come. I hope that this book may inspire many such delicious and happy occasions.

Cooking for Occasions

CHRISTMAS DINNER

As this is the one meal people always ask vegetarians about, perhaps I'd better take it as a starting point and reveal what vegetarians – this vegetarian, at any rate – do eat for Christmas dinner.

Actually, this is a particularly difficult meal to plan because it is so strongly associated with the eating of turkey. So people are much more conscious of not having turkey at a vegetarian Christmas dinner than they would be of not having meat at a dinner party, when they are not expecting any particular dish.

For this reason I am inclined to keep Christmas dinner as traditional as possible in other ways, with sprouts, chestnuts, roast potatoes, cranberry sauce and bread sauce, but with a savoury nut loaf instead of turkey, followed by Christmas

pudding and brandy butter. I find it difficult to resist changing
the savoury loaf in some way every year, but the one which my
family like best and which they always ask me to make is pine
nutmeat with herb stuffing: the stuffing also provides another
familiar Christmas flavour.

This is not a difficult meal to organise because the nutmeat
can be made up to two days in advance and kept, well covered,
in the fridge; or it can be stored in a deep freeze for up to two
months. It has the advantage of being easier to cook than turkey
because it isn't so big and only takes an hour or so. It will cook
perfectly towards the bottom of quite a hot oven with the
potatoes roasting in their own tin above. The traditional
pudding is of course usually made in advance, too; the brandy
or rum butter can be made several days ahead and kept, again
very well covered, in the fridge. It's always nice to offer an
alternative pudding which the children will like and ice cream
is usually the most popular, but that too can be made
beforehand.

This just leaves the first course. Usually, when planning a
dinner party, for instance, I rather like to create an element of
surprise – to produce something a bit unusual which startles
people a little and makes them take notice of the food. But at
Christmas I don't think it's worth it: there are just too many
other distractions, and so a simple, refreshing fruity starter, to
calm people down and get them ready for the rest of the meal,
is best. My suggested menu is:

pineapple wedges
pine nutmeat with herb stuffing
special wine sauce · bread sauce · cranberry and apple sauce
roast potatoes · sprouts with chestnuts
Christmas pudding with brandy butter
or
vanilla ice cream
with optional hot chestnut and brandy sauce

An alternative to the pine nutmeat with herb stuffing would be
the chestnut, sage and wine loaf which brings the seasonal taste
of chestnuts but in a slightly different form from usual. My own
favourite menu would be based around the walnut pâté en

croûte which is a moist, tasty nutmeat encased in golden flaky pastry. This would be best served with buttered baby new potatoes and sprouts, or a purée of Brussels sprouts, which is a useful way to serve them as it cuts out the need for extra sauces.

Of course there is a good deal more to Christmas cooking than this one meal and it's helpful to have several other main dishes (and puddings if possible) prepared and stored in the fridge or freezer, ready to be cooked when required. The kind of dishes which are most useful for this are described in the section on informal lunch and supper parties, pages 18–19.

DINNER PARTIES

A dinner party is more fun to plan than Christmas dinner because you have much greater freedom with the choice of dishes and, with any luck, people will be more interested in the food, anyway! I find six people, or at the most eight, is the right number for this kind of entertaining and I usually plan a meal based on three or possibly four courses plus cheese. I certainly think it is helpful to make at least one of the courses, and preferably two, consist of dishes which can be prepared more or less completely in advance. In fact, although I do not mind doing a fair amount of advance preparation, I am happiest with meals which require the minimum of attention at the time of the dinner party so that I can relax, knowing that everything is going to go smoothly.

It's very helpful to plan a first course which can already be in place when people come to the table – for example, any of the dips, with crudités or melba toast (which is easier than hot fingers of toast because it can be made in advance); artichokes served cold with soured cream filling; surprise avocados; or, for a summer dinner party, when you want something spectacular, grapefruit rose baskets. Another starter which will get people talking is the stripy pâté which consists of several layers of different coloured mixtures chilled in a loaf tin and served in slices. And if you don't mind doing a little last-minute preparation, the hot avocado tartlets make another mouth-watering and quite unusual starter, as do the little mushroom patties with their light cheese pastry.

The final choice of starter will probably be governed by the main course you are serving and, in fact, unless you do want to have a particular starter for some reason, it's probably best to start by deciding on the main course and then build the rest of the meal around that.

An easy way of producing a comparatively conventional main course is to base it around a savoury loaf, as for Christmas dinner, with accompanying sauces and cooked vegetables. The walnut pâté en croûte, flaky mushroom roll and, in the summer, stuffed marrow baked with thyme, are possibilities. As they are all quite rich, I would be inclined to serve them with fairly simply cooked vegetables such as mangetout peas, baby carrots and light mashed potatoes or tiny new potatoes with butter and chopped parsley. Or, as I mentioned before, a vegetable purée is a good choice as it is light and, being moist, eliminates the need for sauces, as does a well-flavoured ratatouille.

Other special main courses which I like very much, although they need some last-minute attention, are the spinach roulade which goes very well after one of the more substantial main courses such as the hot tartlets; and also hot avocado with wine stuffing, delicious served with wine sauce, lemon potatoes and a hot, cooked vegetable. This needs some care as it is not good if overcooked.

The pudding can certainly be made beforehand because there are so many delicious cold ones to choose from. Sorbet is always good after a rich meal, especially if it can be served in an interesting way. The two-colour melon sorbet with crunchy crystallised mint leaves is lovely, so is the strawberry sorbet served in a 'cup' of sliced green kiwi fruit, and rose sorbet, because of its unusual perfumed flavour. Don't forget to take these out of the freezer at least an hour before you want to serve them. I usually get the sorbet out well in advance and stand it in the kitchen until it just about reaches the right kind of consistency and then put it in the coldest part of the fridge (but not in the ice compartment). I keep a check on it during the meal, getting it out of the fridge again if necessary.

Fruit puddings are also refreshing after a rich meal; raspberries in redcurrant jelly or kiwi fruit in grape jelly, stuffed pineapple halves, or peaches in strawberry purée are all good. Sweet pastry dishes are also very popular, especially with men, and, if I can, I usually offer one as an alternative to the lighter puddings: hot blackcurrant lattice with lemon pastry or jewelled fruit flan, for instance. Or, for sheer indulgence, though not after a very rich main course, almond and chocolate flan.

Most people like some cheese at the end of the meal, either before or after the pudding course, and here it's probably best just to offer one or at most two really good cheeses, such as a perfect wedge of Brie and a piece of properly matured Cheddar, followed by plenty of good coffee, black or with cream.

Here are some suggested menus:

artichokes with soured cream filling
walnut pâté en croûte
new potatoes with butter and parsley
purée of Brussels sprouts *or* ratatouille
salad of Chinese leaves with spring onions
stuffed pineapple halves

*

stripy pâté with melba toast
flaky mushroom roll · yoghurt and spring onion sauce
chicory and walnut salad
strawberry cheesecake *or* special fruit salad

*

grapefruit rose baskets
stuffed marrow baked with thyme
purée of potatoes and turnip · buttered baby carrots
herby green salad
jewelled fruit flan *or* raspberry ice cream

*

hot avocado tartlets
spinach roulade · lemon potatoes
braised cucumber with walnuts
salad of Chinese leaves with spring onions
peaches in strawberry purée with crisp biscuits

*

17

bean and black olive pâté with melba toast
hot avocado with wine stuffing
puréed potatoes with cream, butter and lots of black pepper
Chinese cabbage with spring onions · carrots
rose *or* melon sorbet
or blackcurrant lattice flan with lemon pastry

INFORMAL LUNCHES AND SUPPERS

This is the kind of easy-going entertaining when you invite a group of people for supper or Sunday lunch and you either eat in the kitchen or people serve themselves from dishes laid out on the sideboard, standing and chatting as they eat or sitting where best they can.

I don't think a starter is necessarily called for, though one or two different dips with lots of crudités or melba toast, or if it's a cold day, some hot soup and rolls or garlic bread, make a good beginning.

For the main course I go for dishes which are self-contained and don't need fiddly sauces and accompaniments and which, preferably, can be served with just a good green salad. Favourites are special pizza, which is always a success when it's brought out of the oven with the white cheese melting over the colourful vegetable topping; mushroom rice with almond and red pepper; lentil lasagne; baked pancakes with leeks and a light cheesy topping. A flan, such as the colourful aubergine, red pepper and cheese, or cauliflower with Stilton, is also very good for this kind of entertaining, perhaps with some hot buttered new potatoes as well as the salad.

It's a good idea to offer a choice of pudding. If the party is at lunch time and includes children, I would be inclined to offer home-made vanilla ice cream as one possibility because this is something that most of them are sure to like. To go with this, I would suggest a choice of either a fruity pudding such as special fruit salad or pears in cider with ginger, and something a bit more substantial such as Bakewell tart, strawberry cheesecake or cheesecake on a chocolate base. For a real celebration, raspberry meringue gâteau is always a treat.

Some suggested menus might be:

tomato and fresh basil soup with cream and garlic bread
aubergine, red pepper and cheese flan
or cauliflower, Stilton and walnut flan
new potatoes · chunky mixed salad bowl
vanilla *or* chestnut ice cream · *or* special fruit salad

*

melon halves with strawberries
special pizza · herby green salad
cheesecake on a chocolate base *or* almond and chocolate flan
or raspberry meringue gâteau

*

carrot, apple and chervil soup with warm wholewheat rolls
baked pancakes with leeks *or* lentil lasagne
herby green salad
Bakewell tart *or* strawberry cheesecake

*

Cheddar cheese and red wine dip *or* Stilton pâté
with melba toast, hot French bread *or* crudités
mushroom rice with almonds and red pepper · chunky mixed
salad bowl
pears in cider with ginger · home-made vanilla ice cream
or blackcurrant lattice tart with lemon pastry

MEALS TO COME BACK TO

I am thinking here of those occasions when you go out with
family and friends perhaps for a Sunday walk and want to come
back to the delicious aroma of something cooking in the oven.
Or those times when you've been out to some evening function
and you want to come back and find a meal all ready, or one
which needs the minimum of attention.

Three dishes which will cook slowly in the oven without
attention are butter bean and cider casserole which, if you add
potatoes, only needs a crisp, refreshing salad to go with it; the
stripy vegetable pie which is delicious with a cold, creamy,
sharp-tasting sauce and a green salad; and the mushroom
pudding which will steam gently away in the oven if you set it
in a large casserole or roasting tin containing boiling water and
put some foil over the top. Red cabbage casserole can cook in

the oven beside the mushroom pudding and the two together make a lovely filling meal to come home to after a brisk walk on a chilly day. You could even put a spiced plum crumble in the oven at the same time if it's going to be a very long walk on a cold day and there are hungry boys in the party! Alternatively, if you prefer something lighter, I suggest one of the cold fruity puddings – perhaps kiwi fruit in grape jelly or special fruit salad – which can both be left ready.

Suggested menus would be:

butter bean and cider casserole with potatoes
or serve it with onion rice, baked low down in the oven
salad of Chinese leaves with spring onions
cheesecake on a chocolate base
or biscuits and cheese

*

mushroom pudding
red cabbage with apples baked in cider
jacket potatoes with soured cream
spiced plum crumble *or* kiwi fruit in grape jelly

When you want to come home to a meal in the evening perhaps something a little more elegant is called for. Some kind of a dip with crudités is a good idea because people can start nibbling them with a drink, while you do anything that's necessary for the main course. Another good starter for this type of occasion is a bowl of soup, perhaps celery soup with lovage, soothing green pea or cauliflower soup, with some rolls which can warm through in the oven (see page 196) while you heat up the soup.

For the main course you could serve a choice of two or more different cold savouries such as sliced white nutmeat flecked with capers, asparagus flan or moulded rice and artichoke heart salad, with bowls of different coloured salads to go with them. Choose salads which can be covered with clingfilm and left without spoiling while you are out. Apple salad, cabbage salad with nuts and raisins, red kidney bean, carrot and walnut salad, and tomato and broad bean salad with basil dressing are all possibilities, together with some creamy potato salad.

This can be followed by a good cheese board and a choice of

a light and a more substantial pudding: perhaps raspberries in redcurrant jelly or strawberry cheesecake.

These meals might look like this:

Cheddar cheese and red wine dip with crudités
cold lentil and cider loaf with mayonnaise
asparagus flan
potato salad · tomato and broad bean salad
carrot, apple and lovage salad
raspberries in redcurrant jelly · jewelled fruit flan

*

celery and lovage soup with warm rolls
moulded rice and artichoke heart salad
white nutmeat with capers · mayonnaise
cabbage salad with nuts and raisins
butter bean, tomato and olive salad
apple salad
strawberry cheesecake · special fruit salad

LUNCHES AND SUPPERS FOR TWO

When you have a friend to lunch or supper and you have to do all the work yourself and are unable to concentrate fully on what you're doing, a simple menu is called for and, unless you're caught on the spur of the moment, some advance preparation is essential.

Suitable first courses include avocados served with a well-made vinaigrette; melon halves with strawberries; Stilton or bean and olive pâté which can both be made ahead – and for just two it would be practical to serve them with fingers of fresh hot toast. One of my favourite starters is aubergine fritters which, though a bit of trouble, is practical when you're only cooking for two. You can do all the main preparation beforehand and then fry them just before you eat, while you drink and chat.

My very favourite main course for two is cheese fondue, but I feel this is more a supper- than a lunch-time dish. If you have time to take the trouble, asparagus in hot lemon mayonnaise or salsify with white wine and mushrooms are superb and need only hot French bread and a crisp, refreshing salad (which is probably best served afterwards) to go with them. The hot avocados with wine stuffing are good for this kind of entertaining too, served with purée potatoes and a quickly cooked green vegetable, but this is a more complicated menu. Lentil lasagne or spaghetti with lentil and wine sauce are easier and very successful, and they only need a green salad to go with them.

When it comes to the pudding, one of the nicest and easiest to prepare is fresh mango. Other possibilities include stuffed pineapple halves, peaches in strawberry purée, apricot jelly with fresh apricots and strawberries, or one of the ice creams.

IMPROMPTU MEALS

I have to admit that making a special meal on the spur of the moment is quite difficult for vegetarians: most of our food does take a certain amount of preparation and there are very few gourmet ready-made foods which we can fall back on.

Provided the circumstances of this impromptu meal allow you to do some preliminary shopping, a meal that's really quick to prepare is good bread, perhaps two kinds if possible; several interesting cheeses; and a large salad bowl with lots of different kinds of easy-to-prepare crunchy items such as Chinese leaves, chicory, fennel, watercress and iceberg lettuce in a well-made dressing, perhaps containing some walnut oil to make it more unusual. Or a juicy tomato salad with sliced, raw onion rings and black olives. Although it's simple, this makes a surprisingly satisfactory feast served with lots of chilled white wine or cider, plenty of fresh fruit for pudding and some coffee to follow.

Another meal which is quick and easy to make can be based on a cheese fondue. Start off with quick hummus and some crudités, or avocado with a simple vinaigrette and fresh herbs if available, and finish with halved mangoes or baby melons, or an interesting fresh fruit salad if you've time. Served with wine and coffee, this makes a very pleasant meal.

A further possibility is to make a tomato sauce from fresh, not tinned, tomatoes and serve it with grated cheese and plenty of carefully cooked spaghetti that's been tossed in olive oil and fresh green herbs. A crunchy, green salad goes well with this and some fruit or good bought ice cream to follow.

It's a good idea to keep one or two cans of interesting vegetables in the storecupboard for these occasions. Useful ones include artichoke hearts, tomatoes, red kidney beans, butter beans, chick peas (which you need for the quick hummus I mentioned), celery hearts and button mushrooms. If you also have a couple of cans of a ratatouille in stock you can make the brown nut rissoles in ratatouille very quickly and, served with freshly cooked spaghetti tossed in butter or olive oil and a green salad, this again makes a good, quick meal.

If you're used to making pancakes, a savoury pancake dish doesn't take long to put together using canned ratatouille with a dash of wine, or chopped canned artichoke hearts for the filling and the quick topping of *fromage blanc*, eggs and cheese on page 154. It takes about forty minutes to cook and only needs a green salad to go with it and some fruit or cheese to follow.

Stuffed red peppers are also quite quick to do, as are the hot stuffed avocados, if you can get some good, ripe avocados. These can be served simply with a light, creamy potato purée.

OUTDOOR EATING –
BARBECUES AND PICNICS

Barbecues are fun in the summer but for vegetarians they need a little planning and preparation as the sausages or burgers for grilling have to be made first from nuts or lentils! The lentil and mushroom burgers work very well and are delicious served with hot rolls or French bread and mustard or chutney. An alternative is to make a savoury loaf and cut that up and grill it: the lentil and cider loaf can be treated in this way because it slices particularly well.

Hot jacket potatoes filled with soured cream are delicious eaten in your fingers out of doors but don't rely on the barbecue to cook them; I think it is much more satisfactory to do them in the oven, then wrap them in foil and just keep them warm with whatever cooking facilities are available outside. To go with these you need lots of good salad: the chunky mixed salad bowl is ideal, or my favourite well-dressed green salad which I am afraid seems to crop up at nearly every meal.

I don't think a starter is necessary for a barbecue, though you could nibble crudités with a dip while the food is cooking. But you do need lots of food and plenty to drink: chilled cider, lager or beer, and some fairly substantial puddings such as Bakewell tart or a good cake seem to go down well.

Here is a suggested menu:

crudités and Stilton dip

jacket potatoes filled with soured cream

lentil and mushroom burgers with mustard, chutney and soft rolls

chunky salad bowl *or* green salad

fresh summer fruits

candied peel, ginger and almond cake *or* Bakewell tart

You could fry a few sliced onions and tomatoes, too, if you felt like it, along with the burgers.

When it comes to special picnics, I think it adds to the occasion if you begin with a starter. Chilled raspberry and redcurrant soup or chilled tomato and fresh basil soup would be very pleasant. With the latter, you could always change your plans and take it hot in a thermos, if, when the day arrives, it looks as though the weather is going to be bad. Apart from this, you could serve melon halves prepared at home and put together again for transporting; or a tangy dip with crudités.

The main course has to be based on salad which can be kept crisp in an insulated container or, not very elegant but effective, it can be transported in a large saucepan with a close-fitting lid and transferred to a bowl for serving. To go with this I suggest Scotch eggs with yoghurt and spring onion sauce, white nutmeat with capers and mayonnaise, and mushroom patties or aubergine, red pepper and cheese flan.

One of my favourite puddings for a summer picnic is strawberries and cream, but a cake or tart of some kind is also usually appreciated as everyone always seems to eat more in the fresh air. Raspberry cream layer sponge would be lovely for a special occasion such as a summer birthday picnic, or, if you can manage to pack it and keep it cool, strawberry cheesecake.

A more practical proposition, perhaps, would be candied peel, ginger and almond peel cake. To go with a picnic, have a wine that's fun and easy to drink, like a sparkling rosé, or some dry cider, lager or lemonade for the thirsty ones.

DRINKS PARTIES, BUFFET PARTIES, RECEPTIONS

For a drinks party which takes place at lunch time, probably at the weekend, or in the early evening during the week, you just want tasty nibbles – food that's attractive to look at and easy to eat when you're trying to balance a drink and chat at the same time under somewhat noisy and crowded conditions. It's best if most of the food can be prepared in advance, though it is nice to be able to bring out one or two hot savouries half way through if you can.

Suggested food might be:

asparagus rolls · coloured pinwheels
miniature open sandwiches · baby scones
mushroom patties · asparagus boats
wholewheat cheese straws
miniature curried lentil rissoles with soured cream

The pastry dishes would be delightful served hot from the oven if you could manage it, but they would also be all right cold. Hot or cold, the pastry needs to be really thin and light and the portions small.

For a buffet party, or something like a wedding reception or christening party, you usually need food that's more substantial and can be eaten easily with a fork. Perhaps the main headache here is how much to prepare. Quantities are difficult to judge; when people are together at these kind of occasions they tend to eat less than you think they will.

My own rough-and-ready way of working out quantities is to think what I would eat myself and multiply it by the number of people who are going to be present! This simple method works very well; remember though that if you offer a variety of salads and savouries people will probably have tiny helpings of lots of different things, to try as many as possible. Here is a sample menu:

miniature curried lentil rissoles with soured cream
deep dish mushroom pie · white nutmeat with capers
lemon mayonnaise *or* yoghurt and herb sauce
rice·salad ring with egg mayonnaise filling
potato salad · red and white chicory salad
red kidney bean, carrot and walnut salad
tomato and broad bean salad with basil dressing
individual assorted jellies: apricot, raspberry and kiwi fruit
thin crisp ginger biscuits · vanilla drops
raspberry cream sponge *or* chocolate hazel nut gâteau

Wine with Vegetarian Food

The same principles apply when choosing wine for a vegetarian meal as for any other type of meal: you need wine with the right amount of weight and body for the kind of food you're serving, and you should get something that you like. There is of course no tradition of what you should or should not drink with nut roast and if you have a favourite recipe it is interesting and pleasant to experiment by serving it with different wines on various occasions to see which you prefer.

Here are a few suggestions which I hope might be helpful as a general guide.

BEFORE THE MEAL

The ideal aperitif is fresh-tasting, even slightly astringent, to stimulate the appetite and wake up the palate ready for the food to come. Most people have their own particular favourite, but a popular alternative to the usual drinks is a crisp dry wine, such as a Chablis, Mâcon Villages or Muscadet from France, a Soave or Frascati from Italy, Dão from Portugal or the spicy German Gewürztraminer, to mention just a few. A pleasant variation is to add a few drops of the blackcurrant liqueur, cassis, to the wine to make the pretty pink drink, Kir. The proportions are five of wine to one of cassis and traditionally the wine should be Aligoté, but any dry, crisp, inexpensive white will do.

These wines should of course be well chilled, and if you serve sherry, that too should be chilled. It is surprising what a difference this makes: a chilled dry fino sherry or the slightly salty-tasting Manzanilla are hard to beat, though many people prefer a medium sherry and you should offer this as an alternative, especially if you are planning to start the meal with a mellow fruit dish, such as melon or pineapple, which go well with the last of the sherry.

Chilled dry white vermouth, especially the French Chambéry, is also very pleasant served with ice and a slice of lemon or topped up with tonic water or equal quantities of apple and orange juice and a sprig of mint to drink in the garden on a warm summer evening.

FIRST COURSES

Having more than one kind of wine during the meal, to go with the different courses, gives a feeling of luxury and celebration. But it's not that extravagant and unreasonable if you are going to need two bottles of wine anyway for a dinner party of, say, six people. The basic rule here is dry before sweet and youth before age. Be careful, too, about serving white wines after red. This doesn't apply to the glorious, honeyed-sweet white dessert wine with which you might wish to round off the meal; but don't serve an ordinary dry or medium-dry white wine after a full, rounded red or the white will seem poor by comparison. If in

doubt, taste a little of the wines beforehand to check that they
will follow each other well: you only have to try a dry wine after
a sweet one, or a cheapish immature one after a good one, to
realise the reason for this rule, and though there are occasions
when it can be broken with aplomb you need to know your
wines well in order to do so.

Generally speaking soups do not go particularly well with
wine, neither do dishes with sharp-tasting vinaigrette dressings,
nor tart fruits such as grapefruit, though sweet pineapple and
melon are pleasant with a medium sherry, perhaps carried over
from the pre-meal drinks.

Creamy first courses, such as the artichokes with soured
cream, surprise avocados, stripy pâté and soured cream dip,
need a fairly full-bodied, dry white wine of the type you might
serve with fish. The wines which I have suggested as aperitifs
would actually do very well and could be carried through to the
meal. I also like an aperitif drink, Manzanilla sherry, with the
tangy bean and black olive pâté and with hummus. It is in fact
a good idea to bear in mind what you are going to have for the
first course of the meal when offering the drinks beforehand.

With the Cheddar cheese and red wine dip and the Stilton
pâté with pears, it would be interesting to serve the wines
suggested for these cheeses by the Wine Development Board
and the English Country Cheese Council: an Italian Barbera for
the Cheddar dip (you could use some to make the dip, too) and
a port, perhaps a Portuguese white or a tawny, for the Stilton
dip.

The various patties and pastries would be enhanced by a dry
white wine but the curried vegetable and nut pâté, and the
miniature curried lentil rissoles, are probably better without.

THE MAIN COURSE

The rich asparagus in hot lemon mayonnaise and salsify with
white wine and mushrooms need a dry full-bodied white wine
or a really dry rosé to stand up to them – the kind of wine you
would put with fish in a rich sauce – and I would treat the
spinach roulade in the same way. Vouvray, Chablis, Sylvaner,
Soave, Riesling and Gewürztraminer are possibilities.

When it comes to the stuffed red peppers with almonds, the tomatoes stuffed with pine kernels and the hot avocado with wine stuffing, which are all strongly flavoured either with tomatoes or herbs, I would suggest a full-bodied wine from an area where these ingredients are used in the local cookery. A Côtes de Provence would do very well. The rich stuffed marrow baked with butter and thyme also needs a robust wine to go with it: you could serve a full-bodied white but I think a red, such as a Burgundy, Bordeaux or Rhône would be a better choice, or a Spanish Rioja.

Coming on to the pastry dishes, dry or medium-dry white wine would go well with the asparagus flan; a red or a full-bodied white with the aubergine, red pepper and cheese flan, while the walnut pâté en croûte needs a Burgundy or claret. I think I'd choose an Italian red, perhaps the Barbera again, to go with the cauliflower, Stilton and walnut flan which is strongly flavoured.

Italian red wine, perhaps a Chianti or Barbera, would also be my first choice for the Italian-style dishes, pizza, lentil lasagne and spaghetti with lentils. A Californian red, made from the Zinfandel grape, also goes well with these, while for the baked pancakes with leeks either a white or red, again with some body. For the mushroom rice with almond and red pepper I would try a Spanish wine, either a full-bodied white or a red. Strictly speaking, I suppose cheese fondue should be served with a dry Swiss wine but I would plump for any good dry or medium-dry white, perhaps a Soave.

Rather as with chicken and turkey, you could serve either a white or a red wine with the nut loaves, though I think the chestnut, sage and red wine loaf, the white nutmeat with capers and the pine nutmeat, with its herby stuffing, on the whole go best with red as they are all fairly strongly flavoured. A claret or its equivalent would do very nicely.

These nut loaves and also the walnut pâté en croute all slice well when they're cold; try them with an assortment of pretty salads and some chilled dry or medium-dry white or rosé wine, or a red for the walnut pâté, perhaps a chilled Beaujolais for a change. And for a summer picnic, something that's light and easy to drink like a hock, perhaps the delicate, flowery

Piesporter or, for fun, one of the many good sparkling wines you can get now, either white or rosé.

WITH THE CHEESE AND PUDDING

Wine connoisseurs suggest serving the cheese before the pudding so that you can finish off the last of the red wine with it before moving on to the pudding and the sweet wine; or you could have the pudding and then some cheese with port. It is certainly a treat to round off a special meal with one of the really glorious, sweet wines but I personally prefer to enjoy these on their own, or perhaps with perfectly ripe, fragrant Charentais melon, simple fresh fruit salad, stuffed pineapple halves or ripe peaches in (sweetish) strawberry purée.

Vegetarian Nutrition

Although nutrition may not be the main thing in your mind when you're cooking for a special occasion, if you're planning meals which exclude meat and fish it's helpful to know a few facts about protein.

Protein in a vegetarian diet comes mainly from four groups of foods:

Dairy produce: eggs, milk and milk products such as cheese and yoghurt;

Nuts and seeds: all kinds of nut, also sunflower and sesame seeds, which are excellent sources of protein. Peanuts actually belong to the pulse group, though they are rich in protein, and chestnuts are a carbohydrate food and are not a good source;

Pulses: the large group of dried lentils, peas and beans which all contain valuable amounts of protein;

Cereals: although often considered merely as carbohydrate foods, cereals do in fact contribute some protein: three slices of bread, for instance, supply nearly a third of the daily protein requirements of an average man.

These daily protein requirements are recommended by the Food and Agriculture Organization of the United Nations (the FAO) and by Britain's Department of Health and Social Security. The figures are revised from time to time as understanding about nutrition increases and it is interesting to note that the amount of protein recommended now is half that stated in the 1948 edition.

The latest figures, published by the Department of Health and Social Security in 1969, suggest an intake of 1.7 grams of protein for every kilogram of body weight for a child, and 0.59 grams per kilo of body weight for an adult. Adult requirement is less as protein is only needed for repair of tissues, not for growth.

This means that a man weighing, say 60 kilograms (150 lbs or 10^1/$_2$ stone), needs 36 grams of protein during the day. This list of the protein content of different foods shows how this can be provided by vegetarian foods:

Food	grams of protein per oz
wholewheat bread	2.3
macaroni, raw	3.0
flour, wholewheat	2.5
rice, uncooked	1.8
soya flour, full fat	11.5
shredded wheat	2.8
Weetabix	3.1
cheese, hard, average	7.0
milk, fresh	0.9 (or 9.0 for 300ml, ^{1}/$_2$ pint)
eggs	3.4 (or 6.8 for 1 whole egg)
butter beans, dried	5.5
lentils, dried	6.8
almonds	5.8
brazil nuts	3.9
chestnuts	0.7
peanuts	8.0
walnuts	3.6
potatoes, old, raw	0.6
cabbage, raw	0.9

From this it is easy to see that the average protein requirement of 36 grams can be met by having, say:

2 large slices bread	7.0g
300ml (^{1}/$_2$ pint) milk	9.0g
1 medium-sized baked potato	3.6g
with 50g (2 oz) cheese	14.0g
and 1 egg *or* 25g (1 oz) nuts or lentils, say	6.0g

(These figures are taken from *The Composition of Foods* by R. A. McCance and E. M. Widdowson, HMSO 1967.)

Another point which concerns some people is whether the quality of protein obtained from vegetarian sources is as good as that derived from meat and fish.

The fact is that all protein is made up of about twenty-two different amino acids which are present in different foods in various quantities and combinations. Of these amino acids there are eight which are said to be 'essential' amino acids because the body cannot synthesize them. These essential amino acids all have to be present at the same time and, if the body is going to use them most economically, in the right proportions. This means that if a food only contains half the necessary amount of one of these essential amino acids, the body can only use half of each of the others, wasting the rest.

The proportions of essential amino acids found in animal proteins, including eggs, are close to the requirements of the body. However, most vegetable protein are short on one or two of the essential amino acids, which means that not all their protein can be utilized.

The good news, though, is that the different groups of proteins – dairy, nut and seed, pulse and cereal – are deficient in different essential amino acids. So, if you mix the protein from two or more groups at the same meal you end up with more available protein than would otherwise be the case: up to about fifty per cent in some instances. This means that if you mix your proteins (as frequently happens naturally at a meal anyway) it's even easier to reach the recommended protein levels on a vegetarian diet.

As far as the planning of individual meals is concerned, it is a good idea to think of the protein of the meal as a whole, and if the main course happens to be a vegetable or cereal-based one, make up any possible deficiency by serving a protein-rich starter or pudding, or biscuits and cheese to round off the meal. In this book, most of the main course dishes are in fact rich in protein, and in the few cases where this is not so, I have given suggestions with the recipe for increasing the protein content of the meal.

Note on Ingredients

Most of the ingredients in this book are readily available, but here are a few notes which might be helpful.

DAIRY PRODUCE

Hard cheese: most hard cheeses contain rennet, a substance taken from the stomach of calves, and although the quantity is small and in the past eating such cheese has been a compromise which vegetarians have had to make, it is now possible to buy excellent Cheddar and Cheshire cheese made with non-animal rennet. I use these for nearly all my cooking – you should be able to get them at health shops, and some large supermarkets are also beginning to stock them. Parmesan cheese is useful in very small quantities for flavouring; it's best to buy a piece if you can and grate it as you need it.

Curd cheese: I find this medium-fat white cheese useful for both sweet and savoury dishes. It has a rich, creamy flavour yet far fewer calories than cream cheese (40 calories per 25g (1 oz) to 130 per 25g (1 oz) for cream cheese, with cottage cheese at 30). If you beat in a little milk to lighten the texture, curd cheese can be used as a substitute for *fromage blanc*.

Fromage blanc: is a light, smooth cheese which comes in a tub and is something between a natural yoghurt and curd cheese. It has a creamy texture and flavour and is only 30 calories per 25g (1 oz). I love it and use it a great deal instead of cream; in fact, I think it tastes very much like soured cream. Incidentally, talking of soured cream, if you want to increase the richness of a dish without adding too many calories, soured cream is a good bet as it has only 60 calories per 25g (1 oz), the same as single cream and less than half the calories of double cream which is 130.

Butter and margarine: I use both butter and margarine in cooking but try to do so sparingly, reserving butter for those dishes which really need its special flavour and only buying a margarine high in polyunsaturated fats. I prefer Flora, Sainsbury's Soya margarine and Waitrose's 'low cholesterol' margarine as they are the richest in polyunsaturates, and also Vitaquell from health shops as it is pale in colour and unsalted.

NUTS

Although these are expensive, they compare favourably with meat when you consider the quantities used. In this book I have used mainly cashew nuts, almonds, blanched and ground for 'white' dishes and with the skins on for 'brown' dishes; pine nuts for the occasional treat – I can't pretend that these are other than expensive; also brazil nuts, occasionally peanuts, walnuts, which I love as long as they are fresh, and hazel nuts. These last ones are greatly improved if lightly roasted before use. They can be bought like this, with their outer skins removed, or you can buy untreated nuts from a health shop and roast them yourself. To do this, simply spread the nuts out on a baking tin and bake in a moderate oven for about 20 minutes until the nuts underneath the brown outer skin are golden brown. You can rub off the outer skins, if you like, but I don't bother normally. Unsalted peanuts from the health shop can be heated similarly. All these nuts can be quickly ground in an electric or small rotary hand grater, in a food processor or liquidizer.

PULSES

Butter beans, chick peas, red kidney beans, continental 'brown' or 'green' lentils and split red lentils all feature in the recipes in this book. With the exception of the split red lentils, they all benefit from being soaked before cooking. They can either be covered with cold water and left for several hours or boiled for 2–3 minutes and then left to soak in the hot water for 1 hour: both methods work well, and it's good idea to turn the beans into a colander and rinse them before covering them with fresh cold water and simmering them until tender. The rinsing helps to make them more digestible.

You may have heard that, under certain conditions, it can be dangerous to eat red kidney beans. The toxic factor is most probably a haemagglutinin which may lead to acute gastro-enteritis if not destroyed by adequate cooking. Soaking and rinsing the beans prior to cooking reduces the haemagglutinins by two thirds (to about the level present in other dried beans, soaked or unsoaked). The danger can be eliminated entirely *by ensuring that the beans are allowed to boil vigorously for 10 minutes* before lowering the heat and letting the beans cook gently until tender. It is safe to use a slow cooker *provided the beans are boiled for 10 minutes* as above, before being put into the slow cooker.

Beans can be deep-frozen after cooking: I usually weigh the beans out into 350g (12 oz) portions so that they are roughly equivalent to the amount in a tin. You should get four of these portions to 500g (1 lb): 125g (4 oz) dried beans should make 350g (12 oz) when cooked.

FATS

Apart from butter and margarine (see under Dairy produce), I use a polyunsaturated vegetable oil for cooking, either soya which is a good healthy general purpose oil, or sunflower which has a pleasant lightness making it more suitable for some dishes. For salads there is nothing to beat best quality olive oil with some walnut or (if you can get it) hazel nut oil added sometimes as a special treat.

FLOUR

I have used plain 100 per cent wholewheat flour in the majority of recipes but I recommend an 81 per cent wholewheat flour (from health shops) for flaky pastry and for some of the cakes and biscuits where you want to achieve a particularly light result for special occasions.

SUGAR

I am firmly of the opinion that this should be given only a very limited place in our diets, but I have used it for some of the puddings and cakes which are intended as treats rather than for everyday eating. For many of these it's very useful to have some vanilla sugar handy, and all you do to make this is break a vanilla pod in half and bury it in a jar of caster sugar, then keep on topping up the sugar with more as it is used.

LIQUIDS

Stock: although vegetarian stock cubes are available from health shops and supermarkets, nothing can replace the delicate savoury flavour of a good home-made stock. Vegetable stock is easy to make (see page 44) and you can make enough for several days at a time and keep it in a covered jug in the bottom of the fridge.

Wine: it's surprising what a difference the addition of a glassful of wine or cider can make to an ordinary dish, giving it a richness which makes the final seasoning so much simpler. If we are buying wine for a special meal and I just need a little for the cooking, then I use that; otherwise I would buy something cheaper, but not too acid or too sweet, and I very often use a dryish cider which gives good results. For some dishes it's useful to have some fino sherry or a dry, sherry-type wine. Small quantities of brandy and liqueurs are used in a few of the recipes.

Vinegar: for sauces and salad dressings nothing can beat a good wine vinegar – I like red wine vinegar best – but for a change you might like to try the trendy raspberry vinegar, if you can get it, for a pleasant fruity flavour.

FLAVOURINGS

Herbs: fresh herbs are of course best, though not always available. I find made-up bags of bouquet garnis useful, also dried thyme, basil and oregano. Of the fresh herbs, definitely parsley and chives, and as many of the following as possible: basil, tarragon, chervil, mint, thyme, lovage and fennel. The last four are easy as they're perennial (you need plenty of space for lovage and fennel but they are beautiful plants), and tarragon (choose the French variety) should be easy but I have never managed to keep one.

I also use a good deal of garlic which I think helps to make vegetarian food tasty; I like those lovely strings of fat, juicy garlic from France but it is also easy to grow yourself.

Sea salt: is easy to get now and fine enough to use without a grinder. It's healthiest to under- rather than over-salt dishes and let people add more at the table if necessary.

Black pepper: I like freshly ground black pepper from a pepper mill, but I also very much like the flavour of a coarsely ground bottled lemon pepper made by Barbour's.

Spices: nutmeg, grated on a small grater as you need it, also powdered mace are the most useful; curry powder and also the curry spices, coriander (whole and ground), ground cumin and turmeric. Mustard is very useful, and I like to have three types available if possible: powdered mustard and two ready-made ones, a mild, whole-grain type which is lovely for adding to salad dressings and for serving with nut burgers and loaves, and Dijon which is useful in sauces and as an easy-to-add flavouring. Hot tabasco sauce is useful for adding bite to dips and cheese dishes.

JELLING AGENTS

Instead of gelatine, which is unsuitable for strict vegetarians because it's made from the bones and hooves of animals, I use agar agar. This is a fine powder made from seaweed and, in my opinion, the best of the vegetarian jelling agents and very easy to use: you just whisk the agar agar into the boiling liquid, a teaspoon to 300ml (½ pint), then let it boil for 1 minute.

Note on Measurements

Throughout this book I've given the quantities in both metric and imperial measurements. As long as you follow the recipe through in either one set of measurements or the other and don't change in the middle, you should find all is well.

The tablespoons and teaspoons used in the recipes are standard size, 15ml and 5ml respectively, and level unless specified otherwise.

The eggs used are always free-range, standard to large, size 3.

METRIC/IMPERIAL EQUIVALENTS

Grams (g)	Ounces (oz)	Millilitres (ml)	Fluid ounces (fl oz)
25	1	25	1
40	1¹/₂	50	2
50	2	75	3
60	2¹/₂	125	4
75	3	150	5 (¹/₄ pint)
100	4	175	6
125	4 (¹/₄ pound)	200	7
150	5	225	8
175	6	250	10
200	7	275	10 (¹/₂ pint)
225	8 (¹/₂ pound)	300	11
250	9	350	12
275	10	375	13
300	11	400	15
375	13	450	16 (³/₄ pint)
400	14	475	17
425	15	500	18
450	16 (1 pound)	550	20
475	17	575	20 (1 pint)
500	18	850	(1¹/₂ pints)
700	24 (1¹/₂ pounds)	1000 (1 litre)	35 (1³/₄ pints)
1000 (1 kilo)	2¹/₄ pounds	1.2 litres	(2 pints)

Note on Measurements
OVEN TEMPERATURES

Temperature	Centigrade(°)	Fahrenheit(°)	Gas Mark
	70	150	
	80	175	
	100	200	
very cool	110	225	1/4
	120	250	1/2
	140	275	1
cool	150	300	2
warm	160	325	3
moderate	180	350	4
fairly hot	190	375	5
	200	400	6
hot	220	425	7
	230	450	8
very hot	240	475	9
	260	500	9

CENTIMETRES TO INCHES

Centimetres	Inches
6 mm	1/4 in
1 cm	1/2 in
2.5 cm	1 in
5 cm	2 in
7.5 cm	3 in
10 cm	4 in
12.5 cm	5 in
15 cm	6 in
18 cm	7 in
20 cm	8 in
23 cm	9 in
25 cm	10 in
28 cm	11 in
30 cm	12 in

Soups

Soup makes an excellent hot first course. It's simple to prepare and requires very little last-minute attention, yet I have found that it's always greatly appreciated and people think you've gone to a great deal more trouble than you have.

Part of the secret lies in presenting the soup attractively: a swirl of cream and some chopped fresh basil make a simple home-made tomato soup look and taste special; some cream and chopped mint add the finishing touch to a smooth green pea soup, while a delicately-flavoured white soup, like creamy cauliflower or artichoke, is delicious with chopped chives, crunchy golden croûtons or flaked nuts on top.

All the vegetable soups in this section freeze well, but I wouldn't try to freeze the chilled raspberry one: it's better to freeze the raspberries and then make the soup quickly when you need it.

VEGETARIAN STOCK

Although you can now buy vegetarian stock cubes, home-made stock is so much better and it is very easy to make. It only takes about 10 minutes to prepare (followed by 1 hour slow simmering) and it keeps perfectly for a week in a jug in the bottom of the refrigerator. You can add some garlic, pepper-corns and other herbs, such as a bay leaf and some thyme, but this is a good basic recipe that works well for most purposes.

Makes about 1.2 litres (2 pints)

1 onion, peeled and roughly
   sliced
1 stick of celery, washed and
   roughly chopped
1 large carrot, scrubbed and
   roughly chopped

1 medium-sized potato,
   scrubbed and roughly chopped
2 or 3 sprigs of parsley
2.5 litres (4 pints) water

Put the vegetables and parsley into a large saucepan and add the water. Bring to the boil, then turn the heat down, cover and leave to simmer for 1 hour. Strain through a sieve.

ARTICHOKE SOUP

Jerusalem artichokes make a beautiful creamy white soup with a delicate flavour which I think is delicious. They are quite easy to peel if you use a potato peeler and are fairly ruthless about cutting off the little lumps. Put them into a bowl of cold water as they're done, to preserve their colour.

Serves 6

25g (1 oz) butter *or*
  polyunsaturated margarine
1 onion, peeled and chopped
900g (2 lb) Jerusalem artichokes,
  peeled and cut into even-sized
  chunks
1.1 litres (2 pints) light vegetable
  stock *or* water

275ml ($^1/_2$ pint) milk
150ml ($^1/_4$ pint) single cream –
  optional
sea salt and freshly ground black
  pepper
freshly grated nutmeg
fresh chives *or* parsley, chopped

Melt the butter in a large saucepan and add the onion; fry for
5–7 minutes until fairly soft but not browned, then put in the
artichoke and cook for a further 2–3 minutes, stirring often.
Pour in the stock or water and bring up to the boil, then turn
the heat down, put a lid on the saucepan and leave to simmer
for about 20 minutes until the artichoke is soft. Liquidize or
sieve the mixture, then add enough of the milk to bring the soup
to the right consistency, together with the cream if you're using
it, and some salt, pepper and freshly grated nutmeg to taste.
Reheat, and serve with some chopped chives or parsley
sprinkled on top.

CARROT, APPLE AND CHERVIL SOUP

Feathery leaves of chervil have a beautifully delicate flavour
which I think makes this soup special. But if you can't get
chervil you could use other fresh herbs instead: tarragon,
lovage or fennel would be good. This soup is also good chilled,
but in this case it is best to use oil instead of butter or margarine
(2 tablespoons).

Serves 4–6

25g (1 oz) butter *or*
  polyunsaturated margarine
1 onion, peeled and chopped
225g (8 oz) carrots, scraped and
  sliced
125g (4 oz) cooking apple,
  peeled, cored and sliced
1 stick celery, washed and sliced

1.2 litres (2 pints) light vegetable
  stock *or* water
sea salt and freshly ground black
  pepper
sugar
2 tablespoons chopped fresh
  chervil

Melt the butter in a large saucepan and add the onion; fry for 5–7 minutes until fairly soft but not browned, then put in the carrot, apple and celery and cook for a further 2–3 minutes, stirring often. Pour in the stock or water and bring up to the boil, then turn the heat down, put a lid on the saucepan and leave to simmer for about 20 minutes, until the carrots are soft. Liquidize or sieve the mixture, and add a little extra stock if necessary to make a fairly thin, creamy consistency. Season with salt, pepper and perhaps just a touch of sugar. Reheat, and serve each bowl with a good sprinkling of chopped chervil on top – the bright green looks very pretty against the orange soup.

CAULIFLOWER SOUP WITH ALMONDS

Cauliflower makes a surprisingly satisfactory soup, creamy and delicately flavoured. It goes very well with the herb bread on page 194, but if you haven't time to do this, hot garlic bread is also lovely. Prepare this in the usual way by making diagonal cuts in a French stick, not quite through the bottom crust, spreading the cut surfaces generously with a mixture of butter and crushed garlic, then wrapping the loaf in foil and baking in a hot oven for 15–20 minutes, until the crust is crisp and the inside deliciously hot and buttery.

Serves 6

25g (1 oz) butter *or* polyunsaturated margarine
1 onion, peeled and chopped
1 medium-sized potato, about 150g (5 oz)
1/2 fairly small cauliflower – about 225g (8 oz), washed and broken into florets
1.2 litres (2 pints) light vegetable stock *or* water

150ml (1/4 pint) single cream – optional
sea salt and freshly ground black pepper
grated nutmeg
2 tablespoons flaked roasted almonds

Melt the butter in a large saucepan and add the onion; fry for 5–7 minutes until fairly soft but not browned, then put in the potato and cauliflower and cook for a further 2–3 minutes, stirring often: the vegetables for this soup mustn't brown or the delicate flavour will be spoilt. Pour in the stock or water and bring up to the boil, then turn the heat down, put a lid on the saucepan and leave to simmer for about 20 minutes, until the vegetables are soft. Liquidize or sieve the mixture, then add the cream, if you're using it, and season well with salt and plenty of freshly grated pepper and nutmeg. Reheat, and serve with some crisp flaked almonds on top of each portion.

CELERY SOUP WITH LOVAGE

The flavour of lovage is often described as being like that of celery: but it is much more pungent and aromatic. However it does go very well with celery and together I think they make a lovely soup. Made with the first of the English celery and the last of the lovage from the garden, it's a perfect soup for a crisp autumn day. If you can't get hold of any lovage, use some of the celery leaves, finely chopped, instead.

Serves 6

25g (1 oz) butter *or*
  polyunsaturated margarine
1 onion, peeled and chopped
outside sticks from 1 head of
  celery – about 450g (1 lb),
  washed and sliced
225g (8 oz) potatoes, peeled and
  cut into even-sized chunks

1.2 litres (2 pints) light vegetable
  stock *or* water
2 tablespoons chopped fresh
  lovage
150ml (¼ pint) single cream –
  optional
sea salt and freshly ground black
  pepper

Melt the butter in a large saucepan and add the onion; fry for 5–7 minutes until fairly soft but not browned, then put in the celery and potato and cook for a further 2–3 minutes, stirring often. Pour in the stock or water and bring up to the boil, then turn the heat down, put a lid on the saucepan and leave to simmer for about 20 minutes until the vegetables are soft. Liquidize or sieve the mixture, then add the lovage, the cream if you're using it, and a good seasoning of salt and pepper. Reheat before serving. Or serve each bowlful with a swirl of cream and some chopped lovage on top.

GREEN PEA SOUP WITH MINT AND CREAM

Frozen peas make a beautiful vivid green soup with a very smooth texture. It looks lovely swirled with cream and flecked with dark green chopped mint, and is good either hot or chilled.

Serves 6

25g (1 oz) butter *or* polyunsaturated margarine – *or* 2 tablespoons of oil if you're planning to serve it chilled
1 onion, peeled and chopped
900g (2 lb) frozen peas
1.2 litres (2 pints) light vegetable stock *or* water
a few sprigs of thyme, if available
sea salt and freshly ground black pepper
150ml (¼ pint) single cream – optional
2 tablespoons chopped fresh mint

Melt the butter in a large saucepan and add the onion; fry for 5–7 minutes until fairly soft but not browned, then put in the peas and cook for a further 2–3 minutes, stirring often. Pour in the stock or water, add the thyme, and bring mixture up to the boil, then turn the heat down, put a lid on the saucepan and leave to simmer for about 20 minutes until the vegetables are soft. Liquidize, then sieve, pushing through as much of the pea purée as you can. Tip the soup back in the saucepan and season carefully with salt and pepper. Reheat, then serve in bowls, swirling a spoonful of cream over the top of each, if using, and sprinkling with the chopped fresh mint.

CHILLED RASPBERRY AND REDCURRANT SOUP

This soup makes an unusual, refreshing starter. Rich ruby red, swirled with soured cream and sprinkled with fresh chopped mint, it looks really beautiful. It can be made very successfully from frozen raspberries and the redcurrant juice can be bought in cartons from large supermarkets and delicatessens.

Serves 4–6

350g (12 oz) fresh *or* frozen raspberries
850ml (1¹/2 pints) redcurrant juice
2 tablespoons arrowroot

lemon juice
25–50g (1–2 oz) sugar
soured cream – optional
2 tablespoons chopped fresh mint

Liquidize about two thirds of the raspberries with some of the juice, then pass the purée through a sieve to remove the pips. Put into a saucepan with most of the remaining juice and bring to the boil. Meanwhile, put the arrowroot into a small bowl and mix to a smooth cream with the rest of the juice. Pour the hot raspberry mixture over the arrowroot cream, stir, then return the mixture to the saucepan and stir over the heat until it has thickened. Remove from the heat and add the rest of the raspberries and a little lemon juice and sugar to taste. Cool, then chill the soup. When you're ready to serve the soup, ladle it into individual bowls, stir the soured cream to make it smooth, then pour a teaspoonful over each portion and sprinkle with the mint.

TOMATO AND FRESH BASIL SOUP WITH CREAM

When it's made from fresh tomatoes with basil from the garden, this has to be one of the best soups of all. If you haven't any basil, use chopped tarragon or chives instead. This is another soup which I like chilled in the summer.

Serves 4–6

25g (1 oz) butter *or*
  polyunsaturated margarine –
  or 2 tablespoons oil if you're
  going to serve it chilled
1 onion, peeled and chopped
350g (12 oz) potatoes, peeled
  and cut into even-sized
  chunks
450g (1 lb) tomatoes, peeled and
  chopped

1.2 litres (2 pints) light vegetable
  stock *or* water
sea salt and freshly ground black
  pepper
sugar
150ml (1/4 pint) single cream
2 tablespoons chopped fresh
  basil

Melt the butter in a large saucepan and add the onion; fry for 5–7 minutes until fairly soft but not browned, then put in the potatoes and cook for a further 2–3 minutes, stirring often. Put in the tomatoes, mix them round, then pour in the stock or water and bring up to the boil. Turn the heat down, put a lid on the saucepan and leave to simmer for about 20 minutes, until the potatoes are soft. Liquidize the soup then pour it through a sieve into a clean saucepan to remove the seeds of the tomatoes. Season with salt, pepper and about 1/2 teaspoon sugar. Reheat and serve each bowlful topped with a swirl of cream and a sprinkling of basil.

First Courses

The first course sets the tone for the meal, whets people's appetite and gets things off to a good start. I particularly enjoy preparing this part of the meal because it's light and gives scope for imagination and fun.

However, on a more serious note, in a vegetarian meal this course does also give an opportunity for introducing some extra protein if necessary, or a complementary protein, to make a nutritionally well-balanced meal. The avocado with curd cheese and cashew nut balls in tomato dressing, the miniature lentil rissoles, all the dips and pâtés, and the tartlets, contain useful amounts of protein, and some of them can be served with salad as light meals or snacks in their own right.

This chapter is divided into four sections: fruit and vegetable dishes; pâtés, rissoles and dips; pastries and tartlets; and sandwiches. The recipes in the last three sections are also useful for drinks parties, buffets and receptions: see page 25.

Fruit and Vegetable Dishes

ARTICHOKES WITH SOURED CREAM FILLING

For this, the artichokes are cooked, cooled and served with a piquant, soured cream and chive filling. They are messy to eat, so finger bowls are a good idea. If you want to reduce the calories in this recipe, you can use *fromage blanc* instead of the soured cream or half and half.

Serves 6

6 globe artichokes
150ml (¹/₄ pint) soured cream
2 tablespoons mayonnaise
2 tablespoons fresh chives, chopped

sea salt and freshly ground black pepper

First prepare the artichokes. Wash them very well under cold running water, then cut the stems level with the base. Next take a pair of sharp scissors and snip the points off the leaves to square them off and make them less prickly to cope with. You will probably need two large saucepans for cooking the artichokes (or you could do them in two batches, as they're served cold). Put the artichokes into the saucepan and add enough cold water to cover them, then bring to the boil and let them simmer, with a lid half on the pan, for about 40 minutes. They are done when you can pull a leaf off easily. Drain the artichokes and leave them upside down in a colander to cool and let any remaining water drain away.

Meanwhile make the filling, by simply mixing the soured cream and mayonnaise to a smooth consistency, then adding the chives and a little seasoning as necessary.

When the artichokes are cold you will probably need to remove the inner prickly 'choke'. This isn't always necessary if the artichokes are young and tender, but you need to open the artichoke and have a look. To do this, take the artichoke and pull back the leaves, like the petals of a flower, so that you can see the centre. Take the soft central leaves in your hand and pull them away – they should come out quite easily – then use a teaspoon to scrape out any spiky centre or choke. Rinse the artichoke to remove any remaining bits of choke, then dry the inside with kitchen paper. Put the artichokes on individual plates, trimming the bases slightly if necessary to make them stand firm, then spoon the filling into the centre, where the choke was, dividing it between them.

AUBERGINE FRITTERS
WITH TOMATO SAUCE

This is one of the simplest ways of preparing aubergines, but one of my favourites, and I think it is tasty enough to serve as an extra course on its own: almost the equivalent of a fish course. The only disadvantage is that the aubergine does need to be fried just before serving, but this is quite a quick job and most of the preparation can be done well in advance.

Serves 6

450g (1 lb) aubergines
sea salt
wholewheat flour
freshly ground black pepper
olive oil for shallow frying
grated Parmesan cheese

lemon wedges
watercress
400ml (³/4 pint) home-made
  tomato sauce *or* soured cream
  and herb sauce *or* mayonnaise
  sauce

Wash the aubergines and remove the stems, then cut the aubergines into 6mm ($\frac{1}{4}$ in) slices. Put these into a colander, sprinkle them with salt and then place a plate and a weight on top and leave for at least 30 minutes. After that, rinse the pieces of aubergine under the cold tap and squeeze them gently to remove excess water. Dip the slices of aubergine in seasoned wholewheat flour.

To finish the aubergine fritters, heat a little olive oil in a frying pan and fry the slices, a few at a time, on both sides, until the outside is crisp and the inside feels tender when pierced with the point of a sharp knife. As the fritters are ready put them in a baking tin which has been lined with crumpled kitchen paper and keep them warm under the grill or in a cool oven until they are all ready. Serve the fritters sprinkled with a little grated Parmesan and garnished with wedges of lemon and sprigs of watercress. Hand round the sauce separately.

AVOCADO WITH CURD CHEESE AND CASHEW NUT BALLS IN TOMATO DRESSING

This is an unusual starter, little balls of curd cheese and roasted cashew nuts served in a piquant tomato sauce with slices of avocado. The cheese balls and the dressing can be made in advance and stored in the fridge so that you only have to prepare the avocado and assemble the dish just before the meal. You can use bought roasted salted cashew nuts, but I prefer to buy plain ones and roast them by putting them on a dry baking sheet and baking them in a fairly hot oven for about 10 minutes, until they're golden brown.

Serves 6

225g (8 oz) curd cheese
75g (3 oz) cashew nuts, roasted and cooled
1 small garlic clove, crushed in a little salt
sea salt and freshly ground black pepper
1/2 teaspoon tomato purée
1/2–1 teaspoon caster sugar
1/4 teaspoon paprika pepper
2 tablespoons red wine vinegar
6 tablespoons olive oil
2 large ripe avocados
juice of 1/2 lemon
2 tablespoons fresh chives, chopped
crisp lettuce leaves and melba toast for serving

Put the curd cheese into a bowl and mash with a fork. Grate the cashew nuts – a liquidizer is good for this – and add to the curd cheese, together with the crushed garlic and salt and pepper to taste. Mix well, then form into 24 small balls, about the size of hazel nuts. Leave on one side until ready to assemble the dish. (They can be made in advance and kept in a polythene container in the fridge.)

Make the dressing by mixing the tomato purée, 1/2 teaspoonful of sugar, paprika and vinegar, then gradually add the oil. Add some salt, pepper, and a little more sugar if necessary.

Just before you want to serve the meal, peel the avocados and remove the stones. Cut the flesh into pieces and put them into a bowl with the lemon juice, chives and a little salt and pepper. Add the curd cheese balls and the cashew nuts. Mix everything very gently so that the ingredients are well distributed.

Arrange one or two crisp lettuce leaves on each serving dish and spoon the avocado mixture carefully on top. Give the tomato dressing another stir, then spoon a little over each plateful and serve immediately, accompanied by melba toast.

SURPRISE AVOCADOS

'Surprise', because the avocados are completely covered in a sharp, creamy, lemon mayonnaise dressing, and it isn't until you slice one that you find the buttery-soft avocado and the piquant herb filling in the centre. You can make the filling and the dressing in advance, but don't prepare the avocados more than 1 hour in advance or they may discolour.

Serves 6

3 ripe avocado pears – they should feel just soft all over when you cradle them in the palm of your hand
juice of 1 lemon
125g (4 oz) curd cheese
1 tablespoon fresh parsley, finely chopped
1 tablespoon fresh chives, finely chopped
sea salt and freshly ground black pepper
3 tablespoons mayonnaise
3 tablespoons natural yoghurt
lettuce leaves
paprika pepper
lemon slices

Cut the avocados in half and remove stones and skin. Brush the avocados all over with the lemon juice. To make the filling, mix the curd cheese and the herbs, season with a little salt and pepper. For the dressing, mix the mayonnaise and yoghurt.

To assemble the dish, put two or three small crisp lettuce leaves on each plate. Press a little of the curd cheese mixture into the cavity of each avocado half, dividing it between them. Put the avocados cut-side down on the lettuce leaves and pour the dressing over to cover them. Sprinkle with paprika pepper and garnish each plate with a wedge of lemon.

GRAPEFRUIT ROSE BASKETS

You may feel this is too romantic an idea but I think you will agree it provides a conversation piece. I have to admit that I love it because it looks so pretty and different and is just the starter for a celebration meal in summer. It consists of whole pink grapefruits each cut out into the shape of a basket (which is quite easy to do); then filled with the flesh which has been scooped out, chopped and mixed with rosewater and a few fresh pink rose petals, which are perfectly edible and taste delicious! For a final touch each basket can be garnished with a small pink rose bud. You could make this in the spring using a few fragrant violets, which are also edible, and leaving out the rosewater.

Serves 6

6 pink grapefruits	sugar
3–4 tablespoons rosewater	rose leaves and, if possible, 6
a few pink rose petals	small pink rosebuds to garnish

Using a sharp knife, make two cuts in the grapefruit about 3mm (1/8 in) each side of the stalk, going half way down the fruit. Insert the point of the knife at the base of one of these cuts and slice round, across the grapefruit until you get to the other cut. Remove the knife, then re-insert it the other side and repeat the process. These two sections of grapefruit should then fall away, leaving a basket shape. Now cut the fruit from the section under the 'handle'.

Remove the grapefruit flesh from the 'bowl' of the basket in the usual way with a grapefruit knife. Prepare all the grapefruits in this way, then cut the white skin and pith from the scooped-out chunks of fruit. Put this fruit into a bowl and add rosewater to taste, a few fresh rose petals, snipped with kitchen scissors or shredded, and just a very little sugar if you think it's needed.

Stand each grapefruit basket on a plate, cutting a slice from the base of the grapefruit if necessary to make it stand up, then spoon the rose petal mixture into the baskets. Tuck a few fresh rose leaves round the base of the baskets and lay a small pink rose bud on top of each basket, or alongside it on the plate.

HALF MELONS WITH STRAWBERRIES

Although it's so simple, I think this makes a perfect first course (or pudding) in summer. My favourite melons are charentais with their fragrant orange flesh that melts in your mouth, but any small, ripe, round melons would do.

Serves 6

3 small, ripe melons – preferably   225g (8 oz) strawberries, washed
   charentais *or* small   and hulled
   cantaloupe, ogen *or* gallia

Cut the melons in half and scoop out the seeds. Put the melon halves on individual plates. Cut any large strawberries in halves or quarters so that they are all roughly the same size. Put the strawberries in the centre of the melons, dividing them between them. Serve with sugar.

PINEAPPLE WEDGES

A ripe, juicy pineapple makes a beautiful starter, especially before a rich meal. Look for a pineapple that's the right size to slice down in wedges, like a melon, and, if necessary, keep it in the airing cupboard for a day or two to ripen up. It's best if you prepare the pineapple just before you want to serve it.

Serves 6–8

1 medium-large pineapple

Slice off the leafy top, then cut the pineapple downwards in half, then cut each half down into three or four pieces. Put the wedges on individual plates, then slip a sharp knife along between the flesh and the skin to loosen the flesh. Slice off any hard core, then cut the flesh down into segments that are the right size for eating easily.

Pâtés, Rissoles and Dips

BEAN AND BLACK OLIVE PÂTÉ WITH HARDBOILED EGGS

The olives give this dish a lovely salty piquancy and the dip is also very good just served with hot toast or thin wholewheat bread and butter.

Serves 6

125g (4 oz) dried white beans: haricot, canellini or butter beans, soaked and cooked; or 425g (15 oz) can butter beans
12 black olives, stoned
2 tablespoons olive oil
2 tablespoons lemon juice
sea salt and freshly ground black pepper
cayenne pepper
crisp lettuce leaves
4 hardboiled eggs
paprika pepper
watercress
lemon wedges

Drain the beans, reserving the liquid, and mash them to a purée – they needn't be too smooth. Stone the olives, then mash them with a fork and add them to the beans, together with the oil and lemon juice. Stir in a little of the reserved liquid if necessary to make a soft creamy mixture, the consistency of lightly whipped cream. Season with salt, pepper and a pinch of cayenne. Chill this mixture until required: it can be made several hours in advance.

Arrange two or three small crisp lettuce leaves in individual small bowls. Cut the eggs into wedges and put them on top, dividing them among the bowls. Spoon the bean and olive mixture on top and sprinkle with a little paprika pepper. Decorate each bowl with a sprig or two of watercress and a wedge of lemon.

CREAMY BUTTER BEAN DIP WITH SESAME TOAST

This is a creamy dip with a tangy flavour. It's an example of complementary proteins at work, because the wheat and sesame complement each other and the beans. If you use tinned beans it's very quick to make and useful for emergencies.

Serves 6

125g (4 oz) dried butter beans, soaked and cooked until tender, see page 36, *or* 425g (15 oz) can butter beans
1 small garlic clove, peeled and crushed – optional
2 tablespoons olive oil
2–3 teaspoons lemon juice *or* wine vinegar

sea salt and freshly ground black pepper
tabasco
lettuce leaves
lemon wedges
watercress

For the sesame toasts

6 slices wholewheat bread
butter

sesame seeds

Drain the butter beans, reserving the liquid. Put the butter beans into a blender, adding enough of the reserved liquid to make a thick creamy purée; or mash them with a fork and beat in the liquid. Stir in the garlic, if you're using it, olive oil and enough lemon juice or wine vinegar to sharpen the mixture. Season well with salt and pepper and add a few drops of tabasco. Chill the mixture, then just before you want to serve the pâté, spoon it into individual ramekin dishes which have been lined with lettuce leaves, and garnish with a wedge of lemon and a sprig of watercress. Serve with the hot sesame toasts.

To make the sesame toasts, set the oven to 200°C (400°F), gas mark 6. Cut the crusts off the bread and roll each slice with a rolling pin to flatten it a bit. Spread the bread with butter and sprinkle a good layer of sesame seeds on top, pressing them in with the knife. Cut the bread into fingers and place on a baking sheet. Bake for 10–15 minutes, until crisp and golden brown. Serve at once, with the creamy butter bean dip.

CHEDDAR CHEESE AND RED WINE DIP

The wine gives this dip an intriguing flavour and a pretty pink colour. It's delicious for a special occasion served with hot fingers of wholewheat toast or slices of crisp melba toast.

Serves 6

225g (8 oz) Cheddar cheese, finely grated
25g (1 oz) soft butter *or* polyunsaturated margarine
125ml (4 fl oz) dry red wine – *or* you could use cider

1/2 teaspoon tabasco
sea salt and freshly ground black pepper

Put the grated cheese into a bowl with the butter or margarine and the wine and beat them together to make a light, fluffy mixture. Add the tabasco, some freshly ground black pepper and a little salt if necessary – it may not need any as the cheese is quite salty. Spoon the mixture into a small bowl or pâté dish and leave in a cool place until required. Serve with fingers of hot toast or melba toast and butter.

QUICK HUMMUS

This is a quick version of hummus, made with canned chick peas. Normally I don't much like the sweet flavour and soggy texture of canned chick peas, but they are excellent for this dip because of its creamy texture and strong flavour. It's another very useful recipe for impromptu entertaining, either as a first course or for serving with drinks.

Serves 6

425g (15 oz) can chick peas
1 garlic clove, peeled and
  crushed
1 tablespoon olive oil
2 teaspoons tahini – sesame
  cream, from health shops

2–3 teaspoons lemon juice
sea salt and freshly ground black
  pepper
paprika
extra olive oil
lemon wedges

Drain the chick peas, reserving the liquid. Put the chick peas into a blender, adding enough of the reserved liquid to make a thick creamy purée; or mash them with a fork and beat in the liquid. Stir in the garlic, olive oil, tahini and enough lemon juice to sharpen the mixture. The mixture should be fairly moist, like softly-whipped double cream. Season well with salt and pepper. Spread the mixture out on a plate so that it is only about 1cm (½ in) thick; smooth then fork over the surface. Chill, if time. Just before you want to serve the pâté, sprinkle it with quite a generous amount of bright red paprika and drizzle a little olive oil over that. Put some lemon wedges round the edge. Let everyone help themselves to a spoonful and eat it with warmed pitta bread or soft, fresh, wholewheat bread or rolls.

SOURED CREAM AND HERB DIP WITH CRUDITÉS

Like the two preceding dips, this one is quick to make. You can use any fresh green herbs or, if none are available, it's also good made with finely chopped spring onion.

Serves 6

150ml (¹/4 pint) soured cream
125g (4 oz) *fromage blanc*
1 garlic clove, peeled and
  crushed – optional

2 tablespoons fresh green herbs,
  chopped
sea salt and freshly ground black
  pepper

For the crudités
a selection of three or more of the following:

cauliflower sprigs; small strips of red or green pepper; fingers of
  scraped carrot; spring onions or radishes, washed and trimmed, with
  the green part left on if it's presentable; sticks of crisp celery or
  chicory.

To make the dip, simply mix everything together and season with salt and pepper. Put the dip into a small bowl and serve with the crudités.

STILTON PÂTÉ WITH PEARS

The Stilton cheese gives this creamy pâté its lovely tangy flavour. I like to serve it on individual plates with slices of ripe pear and a few fresh walnuts, but it would also be very good served in a bowl with a selection of crudités.

Serves 6

150g (5 oz) Stilton cheese
225g (8 oz) curd cheese
4 tablespoons milk
3 really ripe pears, preferably
   comice

juice of 1 lemon
6 crisp lettuce leaves
25g (1 oz) fresh, shelled walnuts,
   chopped

Grate the cheese finely, then put it into a bowl with the curd cheese and milk and mix well to a creamy consistency. Form the mixture into a fat sausage shape and wrap it in a piece of foil, twisting the two ends like a cracker. Chill the roll for at least 2 hours.

Just before you are ready to serve the pâté, peel and core the pears, then cut them into thin slices. Sprinkle the slices with the lemon juice, making sure they are all coated, to prevent them from discolouring.

To serve the dish, put a lettuce leaf on each plate and arrange the pear slices on top. Unwrap the pâté, cut the roll into six slices and put one on each plate on top of the pears. Sprinkle the walnuts on top and serve as soon as possible.

STRIPY PÂTÉ

This dish consists of different coloured layers pressed into a loaf tin and chilled overnight. When the pâté is turned out and sliced it looks most attractive and impressive, yet it's very simple to make. Serve with hot fingers of toast, or some crisp melba toast.

Serves 6–8

For the first layer (yellow)

175g (6 oz) grated
   orange-coloured cheese, such
   as double Gloucester – *or*
   vegetarian Cheddar
50g (2 oz) butter *or* margarine

4 tablespoons milk
tabasco
sea salt and freshly ground black
   pepper

For the second layer (green)

125g (4 oz) curd cheese
1 medium-sized ripe avocado
  pear
1 tablespoon lemon juice

tabasco
sea salt and freshly ground black
  pepper

For the third layer (white)

225g (8 oz) curd cheese

1 large garlic clove, peeled and
  crushed – optional

To finish

6 stuffed olives, halved
4 tablespoons finely chopped
  parsley *or* chives
paprika pepper

watercress
sea salt and freshly ground black
  pepper

First fold some kitchen paper into about eight layers to fit neatly into the base of a 450g (1 lb) loaf tin – this will absorb any liquid which seeps out of the pâté and ensure that it will be firm and easy to cut later. Then put a long strip of silicon paper on top of this, to cover the base and extend up the narrow sides of the tin.

Next make the mixture for the first layer: put the grated cheese into a bowl and beat in the other ingredients to make a smooth cream. Season with salt, pepper and tabasco.

For the avocado layer: put the cheese into a bowl and mash lightly with a fork. Cut the avocado in half and remove the stone and skin, then slice the flesh roughly and add to the curd cheese. Mash the avocado into the cheese, with the lemon juice, until you have a smooth green purée. Season with salt and pepper and add a few drops of tabasco to taste.

To make the third layer, beat together the curd cheese and garlic, if you're using it, and add salt and pepper to taste.

Put the sliced olives, cut side down, in the base of the tin, right down the centre, then carefully spoon the yellow cheese mixture in on top, pressing it down lightly and levelling it with the back of a spoon. Cover completely with the chopped chives in a thick layer. Then spoon the avocado mixture on top and sprinkle with a thin but even layer of paprika pepper. Cover this with the white curd cheese, smooth with the back of a spoon, then press another wad of kitchen paper on top. Put a weight on top and leave in the fridge overnight. (It's a good idea to replace the top layer of kitchen paper with a new one after an hour or so as it will have absorbed a good deal of moisture.)

To serve the pâté, remove the kitchen paper, slip a knife down the edges of the tin to loosen, then invert the tin over a serving dish, turn the pâté out and strip off the remaining layers of paper: the stuffed olives should now be on top, looking attractive against the yellow cheese mixture. Decorate with sprigs of watercress round the edge. You need a sharp knife to cut the pâté into thick slices; this is a slightly tricky operation, so you might prefer to cut it first and serve it in slices on individual plates – lay the slices flat, to show off the pretty stripes and decorate each with a sprig or two of watercress. It's also nice with the yoghurt and herb or yoghurt and spring onion sauce on page 162.

CURRIED VEGETABLE AND NUT PÂTÉ WITH YOGHURT SAUCE

Another easy one to make, this pâté consists of crunchy vegetables and nuts, flavoured with curry and garlic.

Serves 6

25g (1 oz) butter *or* polyunsaturated margarine
1 medium-sized onion, peeled and finely chopped
1 carrot, about 50g (2 oz), scraped and finely chopped
1 stick of celery, washed and chopped
1/2 green pepper, about 50g (2 oz), de-seeded and chopped
1/2 red pepper, about 50g (2 oz), de-seeded and chopped
1 garlic clove, peeled and crushed
1 tablespoon mild curry powder
125g (4 oz) hazel nuts, roasted and chopped
225g (8 oz) curd cheese
sea salt and freshly ground black pepper

For the dressing

5cm (2 in) cucumber
200ml (7 fl oz) natural yoghurt
3 tablespoons fresh mint, finely
  chopped

lettuce leaves
sliced tomato

Line a 450g (1 lb) loaf tin with a strip of silicon paper to cover the base and come up the two narrow sides. Melt the butter or margarine in a large saucepan and fry the vegetables for 2–3 minutes: they should soften a little, but still be very crunchy. Add the curry powder and cook for a further minute. Remove from the heat and stir in the rest of the ingredients. Spoon mixture into the prepared loaf tin – it won't fill it – and smooth the top. Cover with foil and chill for several hours. Meanwhile make the dressing. Peel and finely chop the cucumber and mix with the yoghurt and mint. Season with salt and pepper.

When you're ready to serve the dish, put two or three small crisp lettuce leaves on individual plates. Slip a knife round the edges of the pâté to loosen it, then turn it out of the tin and cut into slices. Place one slice on each plate. Give the dressing a quick stir, then spoon a little over one corner of each portion of pâté; garnish the plates with sliced tomato. Serve the rest of the dressing in a small jug.

MINIATURE CURRIED LENTIL RISSOLES WITH YOGHURT AND SOURED CREAM SAUCE

These little lentil rissoles can be served hot or cold; they make a good starter and are also good for a drinks party or buffet.

Makes about 50, serves 6 as a starter

175g (6 oz) split orange lentils
275ml (^{1}/2 pint) water
2 tablespoons oil
1 onion, peeled and sliced
1 large garlic clove, peeled and
  crushed

2 teaspoons ground coriander
sea salt and freshly ground black
  pepper
flour to coat
a little butter and oil for
  shallow-frying

For the sauce

2 tablespoons natural yoghurt
2 tablespoons mayonnaise

2 tablespoons soured cream

To serve

lemon slices, sprigs of watercress

Put the lentils and water into a saucepan and bring to the boil,
then turn down the heat and leave to cook very gently for 20
minutes, until soft and pale golden-beige. The lentils should be
fairly dry so that they can be formed into rissoles; if they seem
a bit on the wet side, leave the saucepan over the heat for a few
minutes longer, stirring often.

Meanwhile heat the oil in a medium-sized saucepan and fry
the onion for 10 minutes until softened and lightly browned.
Add the garlic and coriander and cook for a further minute or
two, then add the lentils and a good seasoning of salt and
pepper. Leave until cold, then form into small balls about the
size of large hazel nuts and roll each in flour. Heat a knob of
butter and a tablespoon of oil in a frying pan and shallow-fry
the rissoles until they are crisp and brown. They are rather
fragile and so need to be cooked carefully: I find it best to do
only a few at a time. Drain the rissoles on crumpled kitchen
paper.

To make the sauce, simply mix everything together and
season with salt and pepper.

Serve the rissoles hot or cold on small plates, garnished with
lemon slices and watercress; or, for a buffet, put each little
rissole on a cocktail stick and serve on a plate or stuck into a
grapefruit or cabbage 'hedgehog'. Offer the sauce in a small
bowl so that people can help themselves to a spoonful and dip
the rissoles into it as they eat them.

Pastries and Tartlets

HOT AVOCADO TARTLETS

To make these tartlets, chunks of avocado pear are mixed with soured cream (or *fromage blanc* or yoghurt for a less rich version) and heated through in crisp pastry cases. I think it's a delicious mixture of flavours and textures, but it's important not to let the avocados overheat or you will spoil the flavour. However, the pastry cases can be made several hours in advance and just reheated and assembled, with the avocado, at the last minute. I use little pyrex tartlet dishes measuring 10cm (4 in) across and 1cm ($^1/_2$ in) deep; alternatively you could use metal flan tins of the same size. This dish can also be made in a 20cm (8 in) flan tin and served either as a starter or a light main course.

Serves 6

For the pastry

125g (4 oz) plain whole wheat
  flour
75g (3 oz) polyunsaturated
  margarine *or* butter

75g (3 oz) cheese, finely grated
sea salt and freshly ground black
  pepper

For the filling

2 fairly large avocado pears
juice of ¹/₂ small lemon
sea salt and freshly ground black
  pepper
150ml (¹/₄ pint) soured cream, *or*
  fromage blanc or natural
  yoghurt

2 tablespoons fresh chives,
  chopped

First make the pastry: sift the flour into a large bowl, and just tip in the bran which will be left in the sieve. Rub the fat into the flour using your fingertips or a fork until the mixture resembles fine breadcrumbs – if the fat is soft you might find it easiest to do this with a fork – then add the grated cheese and some seasoning and press the mixture together to form a dough. If there's time leave this dough to rest for 30 minutes (this makes it easier to roll out but isn't essential).

Set the oven to 200°C (400°F), gas mark 6, and if possible place a heavy baking sheet on the top shelf to heat up with the oven. Divide the pastry into six pieces and roll each out fairly thinly to fit the little flan dishes; press the pastry on to the dishes, trim the edges and prick the bases. Put the flan cases into the oven on top of the baking sheet and bake for 15 minutes, until the pastry is lightly browned and the pastry feels set and crisp to touch.

To finish the tartlets, reduce the oven setting to 180°C (350°F), gas mark 4. Cut the avocados in half and remove stones and skin. Cut flesh into 1cm (¹/₂ in) dice, sprinkle with the lemon juice and salt and pepper. Mix the soured cream with a spoon to make it creamy, then gently add it to the avocado, turning the avocado with a spoon so that it all gets coated with the cream, but don't mash it. Spoon the avocado mixture into the flan cases, dividing it between them. Pop them into the oven for about 15–20 minutes to heat through, then sprinkle with chives and serve at once.

ASPARAGUS BOATS

These are lovely for a party or as a first course.

Makes 12

For the pastry

225g (8 oz) plain wholewheat
   flour
125g (4 oz) polyunsaturated
   margarine *or* butter

2 tablespoons water

For the filling

12 spears cooked fresh *or* frozen
   asparagus *or* canned
   asparagus, drained
50g (2 oz) cheese, grated
2 eggs

4 tablespoons milk *or* single
   cream
sea salt and freshly ground black
   pepper
fresh parsley, chopped

To make the pastry, sift the flour into a large bowl, and just tip in the bran which will be left in the sieve. Rub the fat into the flour using your fingertips or a fork until the mixture resembles fine breadcrumbs – you might find it easiest to use a fork – then add the cold water and press the mixture together to form a dough. If there's time, leave this dough to rest for 30 minutes (this makes it easier to roll out but isn't essential).

Set the oven to 200°C (400°F), gas mark 6, and if possible place a heavy baking sheet on the top shelf to heat up with the oven. Roll out the pastry and ease it into the greased boat tins – it may be necessary to do these in two batches, depending on how many tins you have. Trim the edges and prick the bases. Put the cases into the oven on top of the baking sheet and bake for 15 minutes, until the pastry is lightly browned and the base feels set and crisp to touch. Cool, then carefully remove the boats from the tins and place them on a baking sheet.

To finish the boats, reduce the oven setting to 190°C (375°F), gas mark 5. Put one spear of asparagus in each boat and sprinkle with some of the cheese. Whisk the eggs and milk or cream, add the remaining cheese and season with salt and pepper. Spoon a little over each asparagus spear. Bake the boats for about 15 minutes, until the filling is set. Sprinkle with chopped parsley before serving.

MUSHROOM PATTIES WITH YOGHURT AND SPRING ONION SAUCE

I make these in shallow bun tins – the kind with a rounded base that you you make jam tarts or mince pies in. They are lovely as a starter, served warm with the chilled creamy sauce, or for a party, without the sauce.

Serves 6

For the filling

15g (¹/2 oz) butter *or* polyunsaturated margarine
1 tablespoon oil
1 medium-sized onion, peeled and chopped
1 large garlic clove, peeled and crushed

450g (1 lb) button mushrooms, washed and sliced
1 tablespoon fresh parsley, chopped
sea salt and freshly ground black pepper

For the pastry

225g (8 oz) plain wholewheat flour
1 small teaspoon mustard powder
175g (6 oz) polyunsaturated margarine *or* butter

75g (3 oz) cheese, finely grated
sea salt and freshly ground black pepper

For the sauce

275ml (¹/2 pint) natural yoghurt
3 tablespoons single cream
3 tablespoons finely chopped spring onions

sea salt and freshly ground black pepper

72

First prepare the filling. Heat the butter and oil in a large saucepan and fry the onion for about 5 minutes, until it is beginning to soften, then put in the garlic and mushrooms and fry for a further 20–25 minutes until the mushrooms are very tender and all the liquid has boiled away, leaving them dry. Add the parsley and salt and pepper to taste. Leave them on one side to cool.

Meanwhile make the pastry: sift the flour and mustard powder into a large bowl, and just tip in the bran which will be left in the sieve. Add a little salt, then rub the fat into the flour using your fingertips or a fork until the mixture resembles fine breadcrumbs – again, you might find it easiest to do this with a fork. Mix in the grated cheese, then press the mixture together to form a dough, adding a very little cold water only if necessary. If there's time, leave this dough to rest for 30 minutes (this makes it easier to roll out but isn't essential). Then roll out the pastry and use a round cutter to stamp out twenty-four circles to fit the twelve shallow tartlets. Grease the tin very well. Use half of the pastry circles to line the tartlets. Set the oven to 200°C (400°F), gas mark 6.

Put a heaped teaspoonful of fried mushrooms into each pastry case and put one of the remaining pastry circles on top, pressing down lightly; make a hole in the top of each to let the steam out. Bake the patties for about 15 minutes, until they are golden-brown.

While the patties are cooking, make the sauce by mixing the yoghurt with the cream and spring onions and seasoning with salt and pepper.

When the patties are done, carefully remove them from the tin and serve hot, with the sauce.

Sandwiches

MINIATURE OPEN SANDWICHES

Open sandwiches look so pretty and I find they make an excellent first course or nibble for a drinks or buffet party. Make sure that the topping is pressed firmly on to the bread or else they can be rather messy to eat. If you're serving these as a first course, allow three to four for each person. These toppings are just ideas; you can of course vary them.

Makes 24–36 small open sandwiches

6 slices of dark rye bread *or* other flat firm bread	butter 6–8 lettuce leaves

Egg and olive topping

2 hardboiled eggs 2 tablespoons mayonnaise	8 black olives, stoned watercress

Tomato and butter bean topping

225g (8 oz) can butter beans 1 tablespoon olive oil 2 teaspoons tablespoon lemon juice sea salt and freshly ground black pepper	1 small tomato, cut into thin wedges fresh chives, chopped

Avocado topping

1 small avocado pear	1 small carrot, scraped and
lemon juice	coarsely grated
sea salt and freshly ground black	watercress
pepper	paprika pepper
2 tablespoons mayonnaise	

Butter the slices of bread and cut each into four or six pieces. Press a piece of lettuce on top of each to cover and make a base for the toppings.

First make the egg and olive sandwiches: slice the hardboiled eggs and arrange them on top of a third of the number of bread slices. Spoon a little mayonnaise over and decorate each open sandwich with an olive and a little watercress.

For the tomato and butter bean sandwiches, drain the butter beans, reserving the liquid. Then make the beans into a dip by mashing them with the oil, lemon juice and about a tablespoonful of the reserved liquid to make a soft consistency. Season with salt and pepper. Spoon this mixture on top of another third of the bread slices and decorate each with a tomato slice and some chopped chives.

Finally, for the avocado sandwiches, cut the avocado in half and remove the stone and skin. Put the avocado into a medium-sized bowl with the lemon juice and mash until smooth. Season with salt and pepper. Spoon this mixture on to the remaining pieces of lettuce-lined bread and top each with a little mayonnaise, a few shreds of grated carrot, a sprig of watercress and a dusting of paprika pepper.

These look prettiest served on a large plate or wooden platter.

COLOURED PINWHEELS

These pinwheels are good for serving at drinks parties and similar functions: they look attractive, like slices from miniature savoury swiss rolls. I like to make two batches, with contrasting fillings.

Makes about 50

about 10 slices from a large sliced wholewheat loaf

For a green filling

125g (4 oz) soft butter,
 polyunsaturated margarine *or*
 curd cheese

4 tablespoons fresh parsley,
 finely chopped
1 tablespoon hot water

For an orange filling

125g (4 oz) orange cheese, such
 as double Gloucester, finely
 grated
25g (1 oz) butter *or*
 polyunsaturated margarine

2–3 tablespoons milk
tabasco
salt and freshly ground black
 pepper

First make the fillings for the pinwheels. Beat together the butter, margarine or churd cheese, parsley and hot water to make a light, creamy mixture. Put the orange cheese into another bowl and beat in the butter or margarine and enough milk to make a soft consistency; add a drop or two of tabasco and a little salt and pepper.

Cut the crusts off the bread and flatten each slice with a rolling pin. Spread half the slices generously with the green butter mixture and the rest of the slices with the orange mixture. Roll the slices up like swiss rolls and if possible chill them for an hour or so. Then cut each roll into about five fairly thin slices.

ASPARAGUS ROLLS

These are one of my favourite sandwich-type party foods: moist spears of asparagus rolled in thin wholewheat bread.

Sandwiches

Makes about 40

350g (12 oz) canned asparagus
   tips, drained

1 sliced wholewheat loaf
butter

These work out well because there are usually about the same
number of slices in a large loaf as there are spears in the tin of
asparagus! Cut the crusts from the bread and roll each slice with
a rolling pin to make it thinner and more flexible. Butter the
bread. Put one spear of asparagus on each slice of bread and
roll the bread round the asparagus. Cut each roll into two or
three pieces so that they are a manageable size for eating. Keep
in a cool place, covered with foil, until needed.

Salads

There are many cooked dishes for which I think the perfect accompaniment is simply a well-made salad, rather than cooked vegetables: the fresh flavour and crisp texture provide a pleasant contrast.

A salad is also much easier for the cook, especially when entertaining, because most of the work can be done beforehand. Although a green salad needs to be assembled and dressed at the last moment, the dressing can be made – I make mine straight into the wooden bowl from which I serve the salad – and the leaves left in a polythene bag in the fridge ready to be assembled in moments when you're ready. Then the salad can be turned in the dressing at the table, by someone else, if you're busy.

Salads made from more robust ingredients such as root vegetables, cabbage and cooked beans can be made well in advance and are useful for parties and other occasions when you want to get everything completely ready beforehand.

Most of the salads in this section are for serving with other dishes, rather than as main salad meals, though the two bean salads and the rice salad are rich in protein and make attractive, simple meals on their own or as part of a selection of cold dishes for a party.

APPLE SALAD

This salad consists of a colourful, crunchy mixture of apples with carrots, celery, nuts and raisins, with a creamy dressing. on top. It's a good salad for serving with warm wholewheat rolls and cheese for a simple meal.

Serves 4–6

3 red apples, cored and finely
   diced
3 large carrots, scraped and
   finely diced
1 head of celery, washed and
   finely diced
50–100g (2–4 oz) walnut pieces

50–100g (2–4 oz) raisins
2 tablespoons fresh chives,
   chopped
juice of 1 orange
lettuce leaves
225g (8 oz) *fromage blanc*

Put the apple, carrot, celery, nuts, raisins and chives into a large bowl and add the orange juice. Stir the mixture to make sure that everything is coated with the juice. Line a large dish or shallow salad bowl with lettuce and spoon the apple mixture on top. Stir the *fromage blanc* with a fork so that it is smooth and creamy, then spoon it over the top of the salad, so that some of the pretty mixture still shows underneath. Serve as soon as possible.

BANANA, PEANUT AND SPRING ONION SALAD

This salad goes very well with a curry meal because it contains some of the things which are often served with curry – banana, salted peanuts, coconut – but putting everything together in one big bowl is much easier and makes an interesting and unusual salad.

Serves 4

2 large bananas
juice of 1 orange
1 bunch spring onions, trimmed
  and chopped
1 medium-sized red pepper,
  de-seeded and chopped
2 tablespoons natural yoghurt *or*
  mayonnaise *or* a mixture

125g (4 oz) salted peanuts, *or*
  roasted and skinned peanuts,
  see page 36
1 tablespoon unsweetened,
  desiccated coconut

Peel and slice the bananas, then put them into a bowl and add the orange juice. Add the spring onion, red pepper and yoghurt or mayonnaise and mix everything together. Just before serving, add the peanuts so that they stay crisp, and sprinkle with the desiccated coconut.

BEETROOT, APPLE AND CELERY SALAD WITH CREAMY TOPPING AND WALNUTS

This pleasant mixture of flavours and textures goes well with a cold nut pâté or nut roast.

Serves 4–6

350g (12 oz) cooked beetroot –
  the kind with the skin still on,
  not the sort that has been
  prepared in vinegar
2 crisp, sweet, eating apples

1 heart of celery
225g (8 oz) curd cheese
2 tablespoons milk
50g (2 oz) walnuts, chopped

Rub the skins off the beetroots, then rinse under the tap. Cut the beetroot into chunky dice. Peel, core and dice the apples; slice the celery. Mix the beetroot with the apple and celery and put on a serving dish or into a salad bowl. Next make the creamy topping; put the curd cheese into a bowl and beat in the milk to make a smooth, creamy consistency. Pour this over the beetroot mixture and sprinkle the chopped walnuts on top.

BUTTER BEAN, TOMATO
AND OLIVE SALAD

This succulent mixture of flavours makes a very good protein-rich side salad, and it also makes a lovely light lunch or supper, served with warm wholewheat rolls or French bread to mop up the juices.

Serves 4

3 tablespoons olive oil
1 tablespoon wine vinegar
sea salt and freshly ground black
  pepper
1 medium-sized mild onion,
  peeled and sliced
450g (1 lb) tomatoes, skinned
  and sliced

425g (15 oz) can butter beans,
  drained; *or* 125g (4 oz) dried
  butter beans, soaked, cooked
  and drained
8–10 black olives

Put the oil and vinegar into the base of a wooden salad bowl and add a little salt and freshly ground black pepper. Then put in the onion, tomatoes, butter beans and olives, and turn everything gently to mix the ingredients, making sure that all the flavours blend.

CARROT, APPLE AND LOVAGE SALAD

The lovage gives this salad a curiously sweet, aromatic flavour which I find delicious. It is especially good with cheese dishes. Lovage is easy to grow in the garden because once you've got it, it comes up every year – a big plant with attractive leaves and umbelliferous flowers. If you can't get fresh lovage, use chopped mint or other fresh green herbs instead.

Serves 4

3 tablespoons olive oil
1 tablespoon wine vinegar
sea salt and freshly ground black
   pepper
350g (12 oz) carrots
225g (8 oz) white cabbage

3 sweet, eating apples
2 heaped tablespoons fresh
   chives, chopped
2 heaped tablespoons fresh
   lovage, chopped

First make the dressing very simply by putting the oil and vinegar into the base of a wooden salad bowl and mix with a little salt and freshly ground black pepper. Next, scrape the carrots and dice finely; wash and shred the cabbage, dice the apples, discarding the cores. Put the carrots, cabbage and apples into the bowl, together with the chopped chives and lovage and mix well.

CABBAGE SALAD

This crunchy, colourful salad is useful for those occasions when you want a salad that can be prepared ahead and won't wilt and spoil. This one actually improves with time!

Serves 4

3 tablespoons olive oil
1 tablespoon wine vinegar
sea salt and freshly ground black
  pepper
350g (12 oz) white cabbage,
  washed and shredded
175g (6 oz) carrot, scraped and
  coarsely grated

175g (6 oz) red pepper,
  de-seeded and chopped
2 heaped tablespoons chopped
  fresh chives, parsley or spring
  onions
50g (2 oz) raisins
50g (2 oz) roasted peanuts, see
  page 36

First make the dressing very simply by putting the oil and vinegar into the base of a wooden salad bowl and mix with a little salt and freshly ground black pepper. Add all the ingredients except the peanuts and mix well, so that everything gets coated with the shiny dressing. Stir in the peanuts just before serving, so that they stay crisp.

CHICORY AND WALNUT SALAD

If you can get red chicory, this salad is lovely made with half red and half white; otherwise use all white chicory, or a mixture of white chicory and Chinese leaves.

Serves 4–6

350g (12 oz) white chicory
350g (12 oz) red chicory
3 tablespoons olive oil, *or*, if you
  can get it, half walnut oil and
  half olive oil

1 tablespoon wine vinegar
sea salt and freshly ground black
  pepper
50g (2 oz) fresh walnut pieces,
  roughly chopped

Wash the chicory, dry carefully, then slice. Put the oil and vinegar into a salad bowl, add some salt and pepper and mix together, then add the chicory and walnuts and turn them in the oil until everything is shiny with the dressing. Serve at once.

SALAD OF CHINESE LEAVES WITH SPRING ONIONS

This salad is made in the same way as the previous chicory one, using 700g (1½ lb) Chinese leaves and adding a bunch of chopped spring onions instead of (or, if you prefer, as well as) the walnuts. I also rather like it with some raisins added too; they give a pleasant touch of sweetness.

FENNEL, APPLE AND CUCUMBER SALAD

I especially like this salad with pasta and with cheese dishes. Small portions served on a base of lettuce also make a good first course, with thinly-sliced wholewheat bread and butter.

Serves 4

1 bulb of fennel – about 350g (12 oz)
3 apples, peeled, cored and diced

½ cucumber, peeled and diced
2 tablespoons mayonnaise
4 tablespoons natural yoghurt
sea salt

Wash and trim the fennel, removing the tough outer leaves and pieces of stem, but keeping any feathery leaves for the garnish. Slice the fennel quite finely. Put the fennel into a bowl and add the apples, cucumber, mayonnaise, yoghurt and a little salt to taste, and gently mix everything together. Chop the reserved feathery leaves and sprinkle over the top.

HERBY GREEN SALAD

A green salad can be adapted according to the season, and is perhaps the most useful basic salad of all. I think plenty of fresh herbs make all the difference and I personally like to make it quite pungent with garlic and onion rings, but leave these out if they're not to your taste.

Serves 4

3 tablespoons olive oil
1 tablespoon wine vinegar
sea salt and freshly ground black
  pepper
1 garlic clove, peeled and
  crushed – optional
1 medium-sized lettuce, washed,
  shaken dry and shredded
other green salad as available:
  watercress, sliced chicory,
  fennel or cucumber, finely
  shredded tender spinach

2 heaped tablespoons chopped
  fresh herbs: parsley, chives or
  spring onions, mint, tarragon,
  basil – as available
1 mild onion, peeled and sliced
  into rings – optional

First make the dressing very simply by putting the oil and vinegar into the base of a wooden salad bowl and mix with a little salt, freshly ground black pepper and the garlic if you're using it. Add all the other ingredients and mix well, so that everything gets coated with the shiny dressing. Serve immediately.

HERBY HARICOT BEAN SALAD

This salad is best made at least a couple of hours before you need it so that the beans have time to absorb the flavours of the herbs. It's good served well-chilled, for lunch or supper, with just some warm bread and chilled white wine.

Serves 4–6

6 tablespoons olive oil
2 tablespoons wine vinegar
1 teaspoon caster sugar
$^1/_2$ teaspoon mustard powder
1–2 garlic cloves, peeled and
  crushed – optional
sea salt and freshly ground black
  pepper

225g (8 oz) dried haricot beans,
  soaked, cooked and drained
2 heaped tablespoons chopped
  fresh herbs: parsley, chives or
  spring onions, mint, tarragon,
  basil – as available

First make the dressing very simply by putting the oil, vinegar, sugar, mustard and garlic, if you're using it, into the base of a wooden salad bowl and mix with a little salt and freshly ground black pepper. Add all the other ingredients and mix well, so that everything gets coated with the shiny dressing. You can add the beans while they are still warm and the salad will be all the better for it, because they will absorb the dressing and flavourings so well.

CHUNKY MIXED SALAD BOWL

It's best if you can find a really hearty lettuce for this salad: an iceberg or a firm Webb's or Cos, so that you can cut it into nice chunky pieces. The other ingredients are largely a matter of personal taste and can be varied according to what is available.

Serves 4

3 tablespoons olive oil
1 tablespoon wine vinegar
1 garlic clove, peeled and
  crushed – optional
sea salt and freshly ground black
  pepper
1 good-sized hearty lettuce,
  washed and cut into chunky
  pieces

4 firm tomatoes, cut into wedges
$^1/_2$ cucumber, cut into chunky
  dice
1 small head of celery *or*
  chicory, sliced
1 tablespoon fresh chives *or*
  spring onions, chopped
1 mild onion, peeled and sliced
  into rings – optional

First make the dressing very simply by putting the oil and vinegar into the base of a wooden salad bowl and mix with a little salt, freshly ground black pepper and the garlic if you're using it. Add all the other ingredients and mix well, so that everything gets coated with the shiny dressing. Serve immediately.

MUSHROOM, TOMATO AND AVOCADO SALAD BOWL

If you can get those small, very fresh, white mushrooms, they make a lovely salad which I especially like served with pasta tossed in a little olive oil and sprinkled with grated Parmesan.

Serves 4

2 ripe avocado pears
juice of 1/2 lemon
3 tablespoons olive oil
1 tablespoon wine vinegar
sea salt and freshly ground black pepper
225g (8 oz) tomatoes, skinned and sliced

225g (8 oz) fresh white button mushrooms, washed and sliced
1 tablespoon fresh chives *or* spring onions, chopped

First cut the avocados in half and remove stones and skin. Cut the flesh into 1cm (1/2 in) dice and sprinkle with the lemon juice. Put the oil and vinegar into the base of a wooden salad bowl and add a little salt and freshly ground black pepper. Then put in the tomatoes, mushrooms, avocado and chives and turn everything gently to mix the ingredients and make sure that all the flavours blend. Serve as soon as possible.

POTATO SALAD

Potato salad is delicious if it's well made with firm chunks of potato in a creamy dressing, and makes a useful addition to a buffet party.

Serves 6, or more if served with other salads

700g (1 1/2 lb) new potatoes *or* firm-cooking old potatoes
sea salt
2 rounded tablespoons mayonnaise

2 rounded tablespoons *fromage blanc or* natural yoghurt
freshly ground black pepper
fresh chives *or* parsley, chopped

Cook the potatoes in boiling salted water until they are just tender: for the best flavour, cook them in their skins and then slip off the skins with a sharp knife afterwards. Cut the potatoes into chunky dice and put them into a bowl. Mix together the mayonnaise and *fromage blanc* or natural yoghurt, add some salt and pepper to taste. Add this to the potatoes, turning them gently with a spoon until they are all coated in the creamy dressing. Serve cold, with some fresh chives or parsley snipped over the top.

RED KIDNEY BEAN, CARROT AND WALNUT SALAD

The grated carrot in this salad gives an interesting colour contrast and the walnuts add texture, as well as providing extra protein. This salad is nourishing enough to make a light meal, with slices of wholewheat bread and butter and some fruit.

Serves 4

125g (4 oz) dried red kidney
  beans *or* 425g (15 oz) can,
  drained
3 tablespoons olive oil
1 tablespoon wine vinegar
1 teaspoon caster sugar
$1/2$ teaspoon mustard powder
1 small garlic clove, peeled and
  crushed – optional

sea salt and freshly ground black
  pepper
1 heaped tablespoon spring
  onions, chopped
175g (6 oz) carrot, scraped and
  coarsely grated
50g (2 oz) fresh walnut pieces,
  chopped

If you're using dried red kidney beans, cover them with cold water and leave them to soak for at least 2 hours; then drain and rinse them. Put the beans into a saucepan and cover with fresh water; bring up to the boil and allow the beans to boil vigorously for at least 10 minutes. Then lower the heat and leave them to simmer, with a lid on the saucepan, until tender – about 1 hour. Drain.

Meanwhile make the dressing by putting the oil, vinegar, sugar, mustard and garlic, if you're using it, into the base of a wooden salad bowl and mix with a little salt and freshly ground black pepper. Add all the other ingredients, except the nuts, and mix well, so that everything gets coated with the shiny dressing. You can add the beans while they are still warm and the salad will be all the better for it because they will absorb the dressing and flavourings particularly well. Stir in the nuts just before serving so that they stay crisp.

MOULDED RICE AND ARTICHOKE
HEART SALAD

This is a pretty salad of rice with pale green artichoke hearts, mushrooms and red pepper, made in a ring-shape with the centre filled with a glossy, golden egg mayonnaise sprinkled with toasted almonds. You could serve the salad more simply, if you prefer, just roughed-up on a plate, but for a special occasion it does look attractive like this and it's not difficult to do.

Serves 6–8, or more if served as part of a selection of salads

225g (8 oz) long grain brown rice
550ml (1 pint) water
sea salt
4–6 tablespoons oil
1 large onion, peeled and
  chopped
225g (8 oz) button mushrooms,
  washed and sliced
2 large garlic cloves, peeled and
  crushed

2 medium-sized red peppers,
  de-seeded and cut into long
  slices about 6mm (¼ in) wide
8 small, flat, open mushrooms,
  washed and stalks removed
425g (15 oz) can artichoke
  hearts, drained and quartered
freshly ground black pepper

For the filling

6 hardboiled eggs
3 tablespoons mayonnaise
3 tablespoons natural yoghurt

75g (3 oz) flaked almonds,
  toasted
watercress

Put the rice into a medium-sized, heavy-based saucepan and add the water and a level teaspoon of sea salt. Bring to the boil, give the rice a quick stir, then cover the saucepan, turn the heat right down and leave the rice to cook very gently for 45 minutes. Then take the saucepan off the heat and leave to stand, still covered, for a further 15 minutes.

While this is happening, heat 2 tablespoons of the oil in a large saucepan and fry the onion for 5 minutes, until beginning to soften; then put in the mushrooms and garlic and cook for a further 20–25 minutes, stirring from time to time, until all the liquid has disappeared.

Heat the rest of the oil in another small saucepan or frying pan and fry the red pepper, for about 5 minutes, just to soften it a little. After you've fried the red pepper, remove it from the oil and quickly fry the eight flat mushrooms, adding a little extra oil if necessary. Drain on kitchen paper.

Oil a large (1.6 litre [3 pint]) ring mould and arrange the flat mushrooms and strips of red pepper alternately in the base. The mushrooms should be put in black-side down, and the red pepper strips should be placed so that they lie on the base of the mould and extend a bit up the sides – you won't need all the red pepper, so chop up what you don't use, also any mushrooms that are over.

Mix all the mushrooms, remaining red pepper and artichoke hearts with the cooked rice and season well. Spoon this rice mixture carefully into the ring mould, pressing it down well. Cover the ring mould with a piece of foil and chill until needed.

For the filling, chop the eggs into chunky pieces and mix them gently with the mayonnaise and yoghurt. To serve the dish, turn the rice mould out on to a large round serving dish. Quickly stir most of the almonds into the egg mayonnaise mixture and spoon this into the centre, heaping it up well. Sprinkle the rest of the almonds over the egg mixture and tuck a few sprigs of watercress round the sides of the ring.

An excellent variation is to use 450g (1 lb) small leeks, cut into 2.5cm (1 in) pieces, cooked and drained, instead of the artichoke hearts.

TOMATOES AND BROAD BEANS IN BASIL DRESSING

This salad is best if you have time to pop the broad beans out of their skins, and the beautiful vivid green looks very pretty with the red tomato and chopped green basil. If you can't get fresh basil, use chopped chives or the tender part of spring onions.

Serves 4–6

450g (1 lb) frozen broad beans
450g (1 lb) tomatoes
2 tablespoons olive oil
1 tablespoon wine vinegar
1 tablespoon fresh basil,
  chopped

sea salt and freshly ground black
  pepper
lettuce leaves

Cook the broad beans in a little fast-boiling water until just tender, then drain and cool. When the beans are cool enough to handle, pop off the grey outer skins. Peel and slice the tomatoes, removing any hard pieces from the centre. Put the oil, vinegar and basil into a bowl and mix together, then add the tomatoes, broad beans and some salt and pepper. Mix gently, so that everything gets coated with the oil and vinegar, then if possible leave for 2 hours for the beans to absorb the flavours. To serve, line a shallow bowl with a few lettuce leaves and spoon the bean mixture on top.

Accompanying Vegetables

The vegetable dishes in this section are mainly fairly simple ones for serving as accompaniments to main dishes, though some of them, such as the braised cucumber with walnuts, and the fennel in creamy egg sauce, make good first courses on their own, and the ratatouille is also handy as a filling for pancakes and as a base for the brown nut rissoles on page 134.

Some of these vegetable dishes, such as the purées, ratatouille and the baked red cabbage, are particularly useful for serving with savoury nut loaves and pies as they are moist enough to take the place of both a vegetable and a sauce, making them not only simple and delicious, but also saving time and effort.

I have also included two ways of doing savoury rice which are useful for serving with vegetable casseroles and spiced pulse dishes.

SPICED BEETROOT WITH APPLES AND CRANBERRIES

This is an excellent mixture of flavours and very easy to make. It's moist and good for serving with a savoury loaf such as the lentil and cider loaf.

Serves 6

450g (1 lb) sweet apples
125g (4 oz) cranberries
25g (1 oz) sugar
1/4–1/2 teaspoon ground cloves

450g (1 lb) cooked beetroot – the kind you peel yourself
sea salt and freshly ground black pepper

Peel, core and slice the apples. Wash and pick over the cranberries, removing any stems. Put the apples and cranberries into a small, heavy-based saucepan with the sugar and cook over a gentle heat, with a lid on the saucepan, for about 10 minutes, until soft and mushy. Mash the fruits with a spoon, or liquidize if you prefer a smooth sauce. Add the ground cloves, then taste and add more sugar if necessary.

Meanwhile rub the skins off the beetroot with your hands; wash the beetroot under cold water then cut it into chunky pieces. Add these to the sauce, together with some salt and pepper. Leave over a very gentle heat for 10–15 minutes to give the beetroot time to heat through and absorb the flavours.

BRUSSELS SPROUTS WITH CHESTNUT AND WINE SAUCE

There's nothing new about the mixture of sprouts and chestnuts, but this is a different way of combining the two flavours: nutty small sprouts served with a smooth chestnut sauce. It's lovely at Christmas or for a special winter meal.

Serves 4–6

700g (1¹/₂ lb) Brussels sprouts – small ones if possible

For the sauce

15g (¹/₂ oz) butter
1 tablespoon oil
1 large onion, peeled and
   chopped
1 small garlic clove, peeled and
   crushed
125g (4 oz) canned chestnut
   purée

275ml (¹/₂ pint) stock *or* half
   stock and half red wine *or* dry
   cider
sea salt and freshly ground black
   pepper

First make the sauce. Heat the butter and oil in a medium-sized saucepan and fry the onion for 10 minutes until soft but not browned. Add the garlic, chestnut purée, stock or stock and wine or cider, and some salt and pepper and cook for a further few minutes, to give the flavours a chance to blend, then sieve or liquidize and adjust the seasoning with a little more stock or wine if necessary. Put the sauce back in the saucepan and keep it warm over a very low heat.

Wash and trim the sprouts. Leave them whole if they're tiny, otherwise halve or quarter them. Put 1cm (¹/₂ in) water into a saucepan and bring to the boil; add the sprouts, bring up to the boil again and cook for 5–7 minutes – until they are just tender. Drain at once.

Put the sprouts into a warmed serving dish and pour a little of the sauce over them, but don't cover them completely. Serve the rest of the sauce separately.

FESTIVE SPROUTS

This is a recipe for cheering up sprouts towards the end of the season when they are cheaper in price but you're tired of them! It's a very colourful mixture that goes well with many main courses.

Serves 4–6

700g (1¹/₂ lb) Brussels sprouts –
  small ones if possible
225g (8 oz) carrots
2 tablespoons oil
1 large onion, peeled and
  chopped
1 garlic clove, peeled and
  crushed

1 small red pepper, de-seeded
  and sliced
1 tablespoon chopped parsley
sea salt and freshly ground black
  pepper

Wash and trim the sprouts. Leave them whole if they're tiny, otherwise halve or quarter them. Scrape the carrots and cut into 6mm (¹/₄ in) dice. Put 1cm (¹/₂ in) water into a saucepan and bring to the boil; add the sprouts and carrots, bring up to the boil again and cook for 5–7 minutes – until the vegetables are just tender. Drain at once.

Meanwhile heat the oil in a medium-sized saucepan and fry the onion, garlic and red pepper for about 7 minutes, until tender. Add this vegetable mixture to the sprouts and carrots, together with some salt and pepper to taste.

PURÉE OF BRUSSELS SPROUTS

This is an excellent way of serving the larger Brussels sprouts; it's light and delicate in flavour. For a less rich version you can use a little of the cooking liquid or some milk instead of some or all of the cream.

Serves 4–6

700g (1¹/₂ lb) Brussels sprouts
15g (¹/₂ oz) butter
150ml (¹/₄ pint) single cream

sea salt and freshly ground black
  pepper
grated nutmeg

Wash and trim the sprouts, then cook them in a little fast-boiling salted water for about 10 minutes, until they are tender. Drain the sprouts thoroughly, then pass the sprouts through a mouli-légumes or purée them in a food processor. Put the purée back into the saucepan and add the butter, then beat in enough cream to make a soft purée. Season with salt, freshly ground black pepper and grated nutmeg. Reheat gently.

BUTTERED CABBAGE WITH GARLIC AND CORIANDER

This is a simple way of cheering up ordinary cabbage: the garlic and coriander make it taste good enough for a special occasion.

Serves 4

700–900g (1¹/₂–2 lb) firm cabbage, washed and shredded
sea salt and freshly ground black pepper
grated nutmeg

1–2 large garlic cloves, peeled and crushed
2 teaspoons coriander seeds, crushed
15g (¹/₂ oz) butter *or* polyunsaturated margarine

Put about 1cm (¹/₂ in) water into a large saucepan, bring up to the boil, then add the cabbage. Let the cabbage simmer gently, with a lid on the saucepan, for about 7–10 minutes, until it is just tender. Drain the cabbage well in a colander, then put it back in the saucepan and add salt, freshly ground pepper and grated nutmeg to taste. Mix the crushed garlic, coriander and butter or margarine together, then add this to the cabbage, mixing it round well. Serve at once.

CHINESE CABBAGE WITH SPRING ONIONS

If you prepare the cabbage and spring onions in advance and keep them in a polythene bag in the fridge, this dish can be made very quickly, in about 5 minutes, just before the meal.

Serves 4–6

1 Chinese cabbage, about
  700–900g (1¹/₂–2 lb)
1 large bunch spring onions
2 tablespoons oil
1 tablespoon fresh parsley,
  chopped

sea salt and freshly ground black
  pepper
sugar

Wash the cabbage and shred it – not too finely. Wash, trim and chop the spring onions, keeping as much of the green part as seems reasonable. All this can be done in advance. Just before the meal, heat the oil in a fairly large saucepan and add the cabbage and spring onions. Turn them in the oil, over a fairly high heat for about 3 minutes, until the cabbage has softened just a little but is still crisp. Add the chopped parsley and some salt, pepper and perhaps a dash of sugar to taste. Serve at once

---

RED CABBAGE WITH
APPLES BAKED IN CIDER

Red cabbage makes an easy-going vegetable dish because it will cook gently in the oven without any attention and is so moist and juicy that it means you don't need to serve a sauce with the meal. The fruity cider goes particularly well with the apples and cabbage, but it would also be good made with red wine, or you could leave out the alcohol altogether and use stock or water.

700g (1¹/₂ lb) red cabbage
2 large onions, peeled and
  chopped
2 large cooking apples, peeled,
  cored and chopped
3 tablespoons oil

275ml (¹/₂ pint) sweet *or* dry
  cider
1¹/₂ teaspoons sea salt
freshly ground black pepper
1 teaspoon sugar

Serves 4–6

Shred the cabbage with a sharp knife, cutting out and discarding any hard central core. Put the cabbage into a large saucepan, cover with cold water and bring to the boil; then drain the cabbage in a colander.

Meanwhile fry the onions and apples in the oil in a large saucepan for 5–10 minutes. Add the cabbage, cider and some salt, pepper and sugar to taste. Bring up to the boil, then either turn the heat down low and leave the cabbage to cook very gently, with a lid on the saucepan, for about 1½ hours; or transfer the mixture to an ovenproof casserole, cover with a lid and bake in a warm oven, 160°C (325°F), gas mark 3, for about 2 hours. Stir the mixture from time to time to help it to cook evenly.

This dish reheats well – and I also like it cold.

OVEN-BAKED CARROTS

I find it very convenient to be able to cook a vegetable dish in the oven, to avoid last-minute preparations, especially when I'm entertaining. This is a lovely way of doing carrots and seems to retain all their flavour. If you want to bake these carrots at the same time as something else, they can be baked towards the bottom of a hotter oven if necessary.

Serves 6

700g (1½ lb) carrots – baby new ones are especially nice, but old ones will do
225g (8 oz) shallots *or* baby onions
15g (½ oz) butter *or* polyunsaturated margarine

juice of 1 lemon
½ teaspoon sugar
sea salt and freshly ground black pepper
fresh parsley, chopped

Set the oven to 160°C (325°F), gas mark 3. Scrape the carrots and, if you're using baby ones, leave them whole; otherwise cut the carrots into even-sized pieces. Peel the shallots or onions and halve or quarter any large ones. Use half the butter or margarine to grease an ovenproof dish generously. Put the carrots and onions in this and add the lemon juice, sugar and some salt and pepper. Dot the remaining fat over the surface. Cover the casserole and bake for about 45 minutes, until the vegetables are tender. Taste and add more sugar, salt and pepper if necessary. Then sprinkle some chopped parsley over the top and serve from the dish.

BRAISED CUCUMBER WITH WALNUTS

People are sometimes surprised at the idea of cooking cucumber, but it's delicious, tender and palest green, with a delicate flavour.

Serves 6

2 large cucumbers
sea salt
25g (1 oz) butter *or*
    polyunsaturated margarine
275ml (^{1}/2 pint) water

1 tablespoon lemon juice
1 bay leaf
6 peppercorns
25g (1 oz) walnut pieces,
    coarsely chopped

Peel the cucumbers, cut them into 5cm (2 in) chunks, then cut each chunk down into quarters. Put the chunks into a colander, sprinkle with salt and leave under a weight for about 30 minutes to draw out the excess liquid. Drain. Melt the butter in a fairly large saucepan, then put in the cucumber chunks, water and lemon juice, bay leaf and peppercorns. Bring up to the boil, then leave to simmer for 10–15 minutes, until the cucumber is tender and looks transluscent and most of the liquid has evaporated, leaving the cucumber glistening in just a little buttery stock – if there is more than two or three tablespoons of liquid, turn up the heat and let it bubble away. Put the cucumber and the liquid into a warmed, shallow casserole or serving dish and sprinkle with the chopped walnuts.

FENNEL WITH EGG SAUCE

I think this creamy egg and nutmeg sauce goes perfectly with the slightly liquorice flavour of fennel. This makes an excellent accompanying vegetable, but it also makes a very good course on its own, perhaps served in little individual ovenproof dishes.

Serves 4–6

3 large bulbs of fennel – about 700g (1^{1}/2 lb) altogether
275ml (^{1}/2 pint) water
sea salt
1 hardboiled egg, finely chopped

2 tablespoons soured cream *or* fromage blanc
freshly ground black pepper
grated nutmeg

Trim the fennel and slice the bulbs into quarters or eighths. Put the water and a little salt into a saucepan; bring to the boil then put in the fennel and simmer for 20–30 minutes, until the fennel feels tender when pierced with the point of a sharp knife. Remove the fennel with a draining spoon, put it into a shallow, heatproof casserole dish and keep it warm. Let the water in which the fennel was cooked boil rapidly until it has reduced to just a couple of tablespoonfuls. Then take the saucepan off the heat and stir in the chopped hardboiled egg, soured cream or *fromage blanc* and add salt, pepper and grated nutmeg to taste. Spoon this sauce over the fennel and serve as soon as possible. Large, sweet onions are also very good done like this.

BUTTERED MANGETOUT PEAS WITH SUGAR AND MINT

For a simple vegetable dish, I think this is hard to beat. Mangetout peas have such a lovely, delicate flavour and are easy to cook. Like ordinary shelled peas, I think they are enhanced with a little sugar and some chopped fresh mint.

Serves 6

700g (1½ lb) mangetout peas
15g (½ oz) butter
½–1 teaspoon caster sugar
sea salt and freshly ground black
  pepper

1 tablespoon fresh mint,
  chopped

Top and tail the peas, pulling off any stringy bits from the sides. Put about 2.5cm (1 in) water into a fairly large saucepan and bring to the boil. Put in the peas and let them cook gently for about 10 minutes until they are just tender. Drain them, then put them back in the hot saucepan and add the butter, sugar, salt and pepper to taste and the chopped mint. Mix gently, so that all the peas get coated with the butter and seasonings.

GRATIN DAUPHINOIS

Here is my less-rich version of this delicious dish: I have found that by using a creamy, low-fat, white cheese, such as *fromage blanc*, instead of some of the cream, you can get a luxurious-tasting result that's lighter and lower in calories than the traditional recipes. I find this a very useful potato dish; it goes well with many things and is so easy to make.

Serves 4–6

25g (1 oz) butter *or*
  polyunsaturated margarine
700g (1½ lb) waxy potatoes
125g (4 oz) *fromage blanc*
150ml (¼ pint) single cream

1 garlic clove, peeled and
  crushed
sea salt and freshly ground black
  pepper
grated nutmeg

First prepare a shallow, ovenproof dish by greasing it generously with half the butter or margarine. Set the oven to 160°C (325°F), gas mark 3.

Next, peel the potatoes, then slice them very finely, using a mandolin or the slicing edge of a grater. Put the potato slices into a colander and wash them thoroughly under the cold tap to remove some of the starch; pat them dry on kitchen paper or a tea-towel. Mix together the *fromage blanc* and cream. Stir in the garlic and a good seasoning of salt, pepper and grated nutmeg. Arrange a layer of the potato slices in the prepared dish and season with salt, pepper and some grated nutmeg. Spoon a layer of *fromage blanc* on top, then cover with another layer of potatoes; continue in this way until all the potato and *fromage blanc* are used, and ending with a layer of the *fromage blanc* mixture. Dot the rest of the butter over the top, then cover with a piece of foil and bake for 1¹/₂–2 hours, until the potatoes feel tender when pierced with the point of a knife. Remove the foil and serve straight from the dish.

This can be baked towards the bottom of a hotter oven if you want to cook other things at the same time.

POTATO AND ALMOND CROQUETTES

This mixture of creamy potato and crunchy almond is delicious and these crisp little croquettes make a good accompaniment to many dishes. They are useful for entertaining because they can be made in advance and then baked in the oven. They also make a light meal, served with a herby, green salad or tomato salad, in which case this quantity will be right for four.

Serves 6 as an accompaniment, 4 as a light meal

700g (1¹/₂ lb) potatoes
25g (1 oz) butter *or*
   polyunsaturated margarine
about 4 tablespoons milk
25g (1 oz) ground almonds
25g (1 oz) flaked almonds

sea salt and freshly ground black
   pepper
extra ground almonds for
   coating
oil

Peel and boil the potatoes; when they're nearly done, set the oven to 200°C (400°F), gas mark 6. Mash the potatoes with the butter or margarine and enough milk to make a light but firm mixture. Add the ground and flaked almonds and season well with salt and pepper. Form into about twelve little sausages. Roll the potato croquettes in ground almonds, so that they are completely coated. Put the croquettes on an oiled baking sheet and bake for about 30 minutes, turning them after 15 minutes, until they are crisp and golden brown. Serve as soon as possible.

POTATOES BAKED IN HERBS

New potatoes are best for this recipe, but it is also a good way of transforming old potatoes. You need to use a really generous amount of herbs so that their flavour really permeates the potatoes and makes them delicious.

Serves 4–6

40g (1 1/2 oz) butter *or*
  polyunsaturated margarine
a good bunch of fresh herbs:
  whatever is available,
  including some thyme
700g (1 1/2 lb) baby new potatoes,
  scrubbed; *or* older ones,
  peeled and cut into even-sized
  pieces
sea salt and freshly ground black
  pepper

Set the oven to 160°C (325°F), gas mark 3. Grease an ovenproof casserole with half the butter or margarine, then lay half the herbs in the base. Put in the potatoes and cover with the remaining herbs and butter. Season with salt and pepper. Cover the casserole and place it in the oven for about 45 minutes or until the potatoes are tender when pierced with a sharp knife. Serve from the casserole, but remove the herbs first.

JACKET POTATOES
WITH SOURED CREAM

These jacket potatoes are delicious with a vegetable casserole, such as red cabbage and apple baked in cider, and they are also a useful addition to a vegetarian barbecue.

Serves 4

4 medium-sized potatoes – about 175g (6 oz) each
a little oil

sea salt and freshly ground black pepper
150ml ($^1/4$ pint) soured cream

Set the oven to 230°C (450°F), gas mark 8. Scrub the potatoes and cut out any blemishes as necessary. Make a long cut down the centre of each to allow the steam to escape and provide an opening for the soured cream later. Rub each potato in a little oil, put them in a baking tin and place in the oven. Bake the potatoes for 1–1$^1/4$ hours, until they feel tender when squeezed gently.

When the potatoes are done, open up the slit in the top by pulling the potatoes apart slightly with your hands and sprinkle a little salt and pepper inside the potato. Stir the soured cream with a spoon to make it smooth, then put a heaped teaspoonful on top of each potato. Serve at once.

POTATOES WITH LEMON

Many dishes are enhanced by the taste of lemon, and one way of providing this is to flavour the accompanying potatoes with lemon. In this recipe, the potatoes are boiled until almost tender, then mixed with melted butter, lemon juice and grated rind and heated through in a fairly hot oven until they're sizzling and golden.

Serves 6

700g (1 ^{1}/2 lb) potatoes
25g (1 oz) butter *or*
  polyunsaturated margarine
grated rind of 1 small lemon

1 tablespoon lemon juice
sea salt and freshly ground black
  pepper

Set the oven to 200°C (400°F), gas mark 6. Peel the potatoes, cut them into fairly small even-sized chunks and cook them in boiling water for about 15 minutes until they are just tender – they should still have some 'bite', so don't let them get too soft. Spread the potatoes out in a shallow, ovenproof casserole dish, then dot them with the butter or margarine and sprinkle with the lemon rind and juice and some salt and pepper. Bake the potatoes for about 40 minutes, turning them several times, until they are golden. Serve at once, from the dish.

GARLIC POTATOES

This variation of lemon potatoes is also delicious. Prepare the potatoes as described for lemon potatoes, but leave out the lemon. Crush one or two large garlic cloves and mix this paste into the butter before dotting it over the potatoes. Turn the potatoes thoroughly two or three times during the cooking time to make sure that the garlic is well distributed.

POTATO PURÉE

A purée of potatoes (or other vegetables) is useful for serving instead of a sauce with dishes which need something moist to go with them. You can make this mixture rich and creamy for serving with a fairly plain main dish; or just mash the potatoes with some of their cooking water and add plenty of butter and freshly ground black pepper.

Serves 6

700g (1½ lb) potatoes
25g (1 oz) butter
150ml (¼ pint) single cream *or*
   milk – optional

sea salt and freshly ground black
   pepper

Peel the potatoes, cut them into even-sized pieces and boil them until tender. Drain the potato thoroughly, keeping the water. Pass the potatoes through a mouli-légumes or mash them by hand or in a food processor. Put the potatoes back into the saucepan set over a low heat. Add the butter and gradually beat in enough cream, milk or reserved cooking water to make a light, fluffy mixture, softer than mashed potatoes. Season with plenty of salt and freshly ground black pepper.

POTATO AND TURNIP PURÉE

Make this as above, using half potatoes and half turnips, or two thirds turnips to one of potatoes.

POTATO AND CELERIAC PURÉE

This is a very pleasant variation. I think it's best made with two parts celeriac to one of potatoes: 450g (1 lb) celeriac and 225g (8 oz) potatoes. Make as for potato purée.

RATATOUILLE

Ratatouille is a useful dish because it can be made in advance and reheated; it is also excellent as a filling for pancakes or with lasagne. The exact composition can of course be varied according to what is available; some cucumber makes a pleasant addition instead of some of the aubergine or courgette.

Serves 6

450g (1 lb) courgettes *or* marrow, cut into small dice

450g (1 lb) aubergines, cut into small dice

sea salt

3 tablespoons olive *or* other vegetable oil

2 large onions, peeled and chopped

2–4 large garlic cloves, peeled and crushed

2 red peppers, de-seeded and sliced

4 large tomatoes, peeled and sliced

freshly ground black pepper

fresh parsley, chopped

Put the diced courgettes or marrow and the aubergine into a colander and sprinkle with salt, then place a plate and a weight on top and leave for at least half an hour for any bitter liquids and excess moisture to be drawn out. Then rinse under cold running water and squeeze out as much liquid with your hands as you can.

Heat the oil in a large saucepan, put in the onions and fry them for 7–10 minutes, until they're beginning to soften, then add the garlic, peppers and the courgette mixture. Stir the vegetables round in the saucepan so that they all get coated with the oil, then put a lid on the saucepan, turn down the heat and leave them to cook gently for 30 minutes. After that add the tomatoes, put the lid back on, and leave over a gentle heat for a further 20–30 minutes. Season with salt and plenty of freshly ground black pepper. Sprinkle with chopped parsley before serving.

ROOT VEGETABLES IN TURMERIC AND COCONUT SAUCE

This is a beautiful dish of orange and gold root vegetables, bathed in a creamy, delicately-flavoured sauce.

Serves 6

400ml (³/4 pint) milk
125g (4 oz) unsweetened, desiccated coconut
225g (8 oz) carrots
225g (8 oz) swede
225g (8 oz) parsnip
2 tablespoons oil
1 onion, peeled and chopped
1 garlic clove, peeled and crushed

1 teaspoon grated fresh ginger root
1 teaspoon turmeric
¹/2 green pepper, de-seeded and sliced
sea salt and freshly ground black pepper

Heat the milk to boiling then pour it over the coconut, leaving it to infuse while you prepare the vegetables. Scrape the carrots, peel the swede and parsnip and cut them into even-sized chunky pieces. Heat the oil in a medium-sized saucepan and fry the onion for 7–10 minutes, then stir in the garlic, ginger and turmeric and cook for a further 2 minutes. Add the root vegetables, turning them with a spoon so that they all get coated with the spicy onion mixture, then strain the milk mixture over them, pressing the coconut against the sieve to extract as much flavour as possible (the coconut can now be discarded). Add the green pepper and some salt and pepper to taste, then put the saucepan over a low heat, cover and leave the vegetables to cook very gently for about 15–20 minutes, until they feel tender when pierced with the point of a knife.

111

SPICED RICE

Not really a vegetable, but I'm including this here because it is used as an alternative to potatoes and goes well with many of the spicy dishes.

Serves 4–6

2 tablespoons oil
1 onion, peeled and chopped
1 large garlic clove, peeled and
  crushed
225g (8 oz) long grain brown rice
1 teaspoon turmeric

3 cloves
3 cardamom pods
1 bay leaf
575ml (1 pint) boiling water
sea salt and freshly ground black
  pepper

Heat the oil in a heavy-based saucepan and fry the onion for 7–10 minutes, until tender but not browned. Then add the garlic, rice, bay leaf and spices and fry for 1–2 minutes, stirring all the time. Next pour in the boiling water and add a seasoning of salt and pepper. When the mixture is boiling vigorously, give it a stir, then turn the heat right down and put a lid on the saucepan. Leave to cook very gently for about 45 minutes, then remove from the heat and leave to stand, still covered, for a further 10 minutes. Fork up the rice gently, removing the bay leaf and spices.

ONION RICE

For a variation of the above, simply leave out all the spices and season carefully with salt and pepper.

Vegetables and Pulses

The main vegetable dishes in this section range from the elegant and summery stuffed avocados and asparagus in hot lemon mayonnaise, to the hearty butter bean and cider casserole, and spiced vegetables with dhal sauce, which are warming and filling for the winter.

All these vegetable dishes are quite easy to make; the spinach roulade sounds complicated but isn't, and some of the recipes, particularly the stuffed tomatoes, avocados and red peppers also cook quickly and are useful for those occasions when you have to produce a meal on the spur of the moment.

The choice of vegetables to have with a main vegetable dish needs care to ensure that the meal contains enough contrast and interest. Sometimes I think it's best to serve the main course on its own or with a simple potato dish followed by a crisp salad.

ASPARAGUS IN HOT LEMON MAYONNAISE

This is a delicious main course for the early summer when you want to make the most of the short asparagus season. The hot asparagus is coated with a lemon mayonnaise mixture, sprinkled with crumbs and heated through just enough to warm the sauce and make the crumbs go crisp. I think it's best served on its own or just with buttered baby new potatoes, followed by a refreshing green salad before cheese or jewelled red fruit flan.

Serves 4

1 kilo (2¼ lb) fresh *or* frozen
  asparagus
6 rounded tablespoons
  home-made *or* good quality
  bought mayonnaise
225g (8 oz) *fromage blanc*
lemon juice

Dijon mustard
sea salt and freshly ground black
  pepper
50g (2 oz) fine wholewheat
  breadcrumbs
50g (2 oz) cheese, grated

If you're using fresh asparagus, break off the hard stems at the base – these ends are too tough to eat but can be used to make a stock for asparagus soup. Wash the asparagus gently to remove any grit. The easiest way to cook asparagus (if, like me, you haven't got a proper asparagus steamer) is in an ordinary steamer; otherwise you can stand the asparagus up in a bunch in a saucepan containing about 1cm (½ in) water and arrange a piece of foil over the top to make a domed lid – this way the tougher ends of the stalks cook in the water and the delicate tops are steamed. Either way the asparagus will take about 10 minutes: it should be just tender. Frozen asparagus is best cooked in a steamer and takes 7–10 minutes.

114

While the asparagus is cooking, make the sauce by mixing together the mayonnaise and *fromage blanc*. Sharpen with a little lemon juice and mustard and season with salt and freshly ground black pepper. If the mixture seems a bit on the thick side, stir in a tablespoonful or two of the asparagus cooking water.

Set the oven to 200°C (400°F), gas mark 6. Put the asparagus into a large, shallow ovenproof dish and pour the sauce over the top. Cover completely with a thin layer of fine wholewheat crumbs and sprinkle with the cheese. Bake in the oven for about 30–40 minutes until heated through: the crumbs can be browned quickly under the grill after this if necessary – the dish should not be overcooked or the sauce may spoil.

HOT AVOCADO WITH WINE STUFFING

This avocado dish makes a delicious, luxurious main course. Make sure that the avocados are really ripe – they should just yield to fingertip pressure all over. It's important to leave the preparation of the avocados until the last minute, and only just warm them through in the oven, though the filling can be made in advance.

Serves 6

125g (4 oz) brazil nuts, finely-grated
125g (4 oz) cheese, grated
50g (2 oz) fine, fresh, wholewheat breadcrumbs
225g (8 oz) can tomatoes
1 small garlic clove, peeled and crushed
1 tablespoon tomato purée
2 tablespoons fresh chives, chopped

4–6 tablespoons fino sherry
sea salt and freshly ground black pepper
tabasco
3 ripe avocado pears
juice of 1 lemon
a little extra grated cheese and breadcrumbs for topping

First make the stuffing: put the nuts, cheese, breadcrumbs,

tomatoes, garlic, tomato purée and chives into a bowl and mix together. Stir in enough sherry to make a soft mixture which will just hold its shape, then season with plenty of salt and pepper and enough tabasco to give the mixture a pleasant tang. Leave on one side until just before the meal – you can make the stuffing a few hours ahead if convenient.

Set the oven to 230°C (450°F), gas mark 8. Just before the meal, halve the avocados and remove the skin and stones. Mix the lemon juice with a good pinch of salt and a grinding of pepper and brush all over the avocados. Place the avocados in a shallow ovenproof dish. Spoon the stuffing mixture on top of the avocados, dividing it evenly between them; sprinkle a little cheese and a few breadcrumbs on top of each. Put the avocados into the oven and turn the heat down to 200°C (400°F), gas mark 6. Bake the avocados for 15 minutes. Serve immediately. (I find it best to put the avocados into the oven just as everyone sits down for their first course – it's important that they should not be overcooked.) They are delicious with purée potatoes and a lightly-cooked vegetable such as baby carrots.

BUTTER BEAN AND CIDER CASSEROLE

This is lovely served with hot crusty rolls or potatoes baked in their jackets and grated cheese. If you've got a large, flameproof casserole dish, that's ideal for making this; otherwise you will need to fry the vegetables in a saucepan first and then transfer them to an ovenproof dish to finish cooking. A variation is to put medium-large peeled potatoes, one for each person, into the pot with the butter beans and vegetables and cook them together. Done like this, the potatoes soak up the flavours and are delicious, but you need a large casserole dish.

Serves 4

15g (¹/2 oz) butter *or* margarine
1 tablespoon oil
3 large onions, peeled and sliced
2 garlic cloves, peeled and
  crushed
450 (1 lb) carrots, scraped and
  sliced
225g (8 oz) dried butter beans,

soaked, cooked and drained;
or 2 x 425g (15 oz) cans,
drained
275ml (¹/2 pint) stock
150ml (¹/4 pint) cider
bouquet garni
sea salt and freshly ground black
  pepper

Set the oven to 160°C (325°F), gas mark 3. Heat the butter or margarine and oil in a large saucepan and add the onions and garlic; fry for 5 minutes, browning them slightly, then stir in the carrots and cook for a further 4–5 minutes, stirring frequently to prevent sticking. Add the butter beans, stock, cider, bouquet garni and a little salt and pepper. Bring up to the boil, then cover and transfer to the oven to cook for 1¹/2–2 hours. If you want a slightly thicker gravy, stir in a teaspoon of cornflour or arrowroot blended with a little stock and let the mixture boil for a minute or two to thicken. Remove bouquet garni before serving.

SPICED LENTILS

This is a simple casserole of lentils baked with butter, garlic and coriander. It goes well with the spiced rice on page 112, the root vegetables in turmeric and coconut sauce on page 111, and a salad.

Serves 4–6

3 tablespoons oil
2 large onions, peeled and sliced
4 large garlic cloves, peeled and
  crushed
4 teaspoons ground coriander
225g (8 oz) continental 'brown'
  or 'green' lentils, soaked and
  drained, see page 36

275ml (¹/2 pint) water
sea salt and freshly ground black
  pepper

Set the oven to 160°C (325°F), gas mark 3. Heat the oil in a large, flameproof casserole dish and add the onion; fry for 5 minutes, until beginning to brown and soften, then mix in the garlic and coriander and cook for a further 2–3 minutes, stirring. Add the lentils and stir them round so that they all get coated with the oil and spice, then pour in the water. Bring up to the boil, then cover and put into the oven for 40–60 minutes, until the lentils are tender and have absorbed the water. Season with salt and pepper.

STUFFED MARROW BAKED WITH BUTTER AND THYME

A whole marrow can be hollowed out, stuffed and baked in butter and herbs, rather as you might bake a chicken. The result is delicious and one of my favourite summer dishes. Try serving it with apple and redcurrant sauce, roast potatoes and spinach.

Serves 4–6

1 fat, medium-sized marrow weighing about 1 kilo (2¼ lb)
350g (12 oz) soft, fresh breadcrumbs
225g (8 oz) butter
juice and grated rind of 1 small lemon
1 teaspoon marjoram

good bunch of parsley – about 75–125g (3–4 oz) – chopped
1 egg
sea salt and freshly ground black pepper
25g (1 oz) butter
a small bunch of thyme, crushed

Set the oven to 200°C (400°F), gas mark 6. Cut the stalk off the marrow, then peel the marrow, keeping it whole. Cut a slice off one end and scoop out the seeds to leave a cavity for stuffing. Make the stuffing by mixing together the breadcrumbs, butter, lemon juice and rind, marjoram, parsley and egg; season with salt and pepper. Push this mixture into the cavity of the marrow, then replace the sliced-off end and secure with a skewer.

Spread the butter all over the outside of the marrow and sprinkle with the crushed thyme. Put the marrow in an ovenproof dish, sprinkle with any thyme that's left over, cover loosely with a piece of greaseproof paper and bake for about an hour, or until the marrow is tender and can be pierced easily with the point of a knife. Serve with fresh tomato sauce or wine sauce.

STUFFED RED PEPPERS WITH ALMONDS

Red peppers are delicious stuffed with a tasty filling of mushrooms, wine, breadcrumbs, nuts and tomatoes. Serve them with puréed potatoes and a green vegetable.

Serves 6

3 medium-large red peppers
125g (4 oz) almonds, finely grated
125g (4 oz) cheese, grated
50g (2 oz) fresh wholewheat breadcrumbs
225g (8 oz) can tomatoes
125g (4 oz) mushrooms, washed and chopped

8 tablespoons stock, red wine *or* dry cider
1 garlic clove, peeled and crushed
sea salt and freshly ground black pepper
a little extra grated cheese and breadcrumbs for topping

Set the oven to 190°C (375°F), gas mark 5. First prepare the peppers: halve them and remove the centre and seeds; rinse them under the cold tap. Put them into a saucepan half-full of cold water and bring them up to the boil, then take them off the heat, drain and place in a lightly-greased, shallow, ovenproof dish.

Next make the stuffing: put the nuts, cheese, breadcrumbs, tomatoes, mushrooms, stock (or wine or cider) and garlic into a bowl and mix together, adding plenty of salt and pepper to taste. Spoon this mixture into the peppers, dividing it between them. Sprinkle with crumbs and grated cheese. Bake, uncovered, for about 40 minutes, until the peppers are tender and the stuffing golden brown.

TOMATOES STUFFED WITH PINE NUTS

I cannot make this dish without thinking of summer holidays in France because it's something I've made so often at the end of a hot sunny day there, with big tomatoes and fragrant thyme from the market. These tomatoes are delicious with onion rice or buttered noodles and a green salad. You should be able to get pine nuts at a health shop: if not, or if you think they're too extravagant, use chopped cashew nuts instead.

Serves 4

4 large tomatoes, weighing about 225–300g (8 oz) each
sea salt
2 tablespoons olive oil
1 onion, peeled and finely chopped
125g (4 oz) pine nuts
125g (4 oz) soft wholewheat breadcrumbs

1 garlic clove, peeled and crushed
2 tablespoons fresh parsley, chopped
1 tablespoon fresh thyme *or* 1 teaspoon dried
freshly ground black pepper

Set the oven to 190°C (375°F), gas mark 5. Wash the tomatoes, slice off the tops and scoop out the seeds with a spoon – they will not be needed for this recipe, although they can be made into a good sauce to serve with it, following the recipe for fresh tomato sauce, page 162. Sprinkle the inside of the tomatoes with a little salt and place them upside down in a colander to drain while you prepare the stuffing. To do this, heat the oil in a saucepan and fry the onion for about 7 minutes, until softening, then remove from the heat and stir in the pine nuts, bread-crumbs, garlic, parsley and thyme; season. Arrange the tomatoes in a lightly-greased, shallow, ovenproof dish and fill each with some of the nut mixture, dividing it between them. Then replace the sliced-off tops, if you like, and bake, uncovered, for 20–30 minutes until they're tender.

SALSIFY WITH WHITE WINE AND MUSHROOMS

Salsify has a delicate flavour, said to slightly resemble that of oysters. I don't know how much truth there is in this, having never tasted oysters, but I do like the flavour of salsify which I think is very pleasant and delicate. Cooked like this, in a wine-flavoured lemon mayonnaise sauce, with a topping of crisp crumbs and a garnish of fresh lemon, it's excellent either as a main course or starter. If you're serving this as a main course, I think it goes best with just a simply cooked green vegetable such as courgettes, spinach or mangetout peas; or just buttered new potatoes, followed by a refreshing green salad before the cheese or pudding course.

Serves 4

1 kilo (2^1/4 lb) salsify *or* scorzonera which is very similar

3 tablespoons lemon juice

sea salt and freshly ground black pepper

6 rounded tablespoons mayonnaise, home-made *or* good quality bought

225g (8 oz) *fromage blanc*

4 tablespoons dry white wine *or* cider

Dijon mustard

225g (8 oz) baby, white, button mushrooms, wiped and trimmed

50g (2 oz) fresh wholewheat breadcrumbs

50g (2 oz) cheese, grated

Peel the salsify or scorzonera roots and cut them into 2.5cm (1 in) pieces. As they're prepared, put them into a saucepan containing 1 litre (1^3/4 pints) cold water and 2 tablespoons of the lemon juice – this will help to keep them white. When they're all prepared, put the saucepan over the heat, bring to the boil and cook for about 10 minutes, or until the salsify feel tender when pierced with the point of a knife. Drain, sprinkle with the remaining lemon juice and season with salt and pepper.

While the salsify is cooking, make the sauce by mixing together the mayonnaise, *fromage blanc*, white wine or cider and a dash of mustard if necessary. Season with salt and freshly ground black pepper. Set the oven to 200°C (400°F), gas mark 6. Put the salsify into a large, shallow, ovenproof dish and add the mushrooms; pour the sauce over the top. Cover completely with the crumbs and cheese and bake for 30–40 minutes, until heated through. (Timing will depend partly on the depth of the dish you've used, but the mixture shouldn't be overcooked or the sauce may separate.) If the top isn't crisp enough, finish it off quickly under a hot grill. Serve at once.

SPINACH ROULADE

This is good served with buttered new potatoes or lemon potatoes, tomato sauce and baby carrots.

Serves 4–6

900g (2 lb) fresh spinach *or* 450g (1 lb) chopped frozen spinach
15mg (¹/2 oz) butter
sea salt and freshly ground black pepper

4 eggs, separated
a little grated Parmesan cheese

For the filling

175g (6 oz) button mushrooms
15g (¹/2 oz) butter
1 rounded teaspoon cornflour *or* arrowroot

275ml (¹/2 pint) single cream
grated nutmeg
sea salt and freshly ground black pepper

First prepare the spinach. If you're using fresh spinach, wash it thoroughly and put it into a large saucepan without any water. Put a lid on the saucepan and cook the spinach for 10 minutes until it's tender, pressing it down with the end of a fish slice and chopping it a bit as it gets softer. Drain thoroughly. Cook frozen spinach according to the directions on the packet, and drain well. Add the butter and seasoning and stir in the egg yolks.

Line a shallow swiss roll tin, 18 x 28cm (7 x 11 in), with

greased silicon paper to cover the base of the tin and to extend 5cm (2 in) up each side. Sprinkle with Parmesan cheese. Set oven to 200°C (400°F), gas mark 6. Whisk the egg whites until stiff but not dry and fold them into the spinach mixture. Pour the mixture into the prepared tin and bake for 10–15 minutes, until risen and springy to touch.

While the roulade is cooking, make the filling. Wipe and slice the mushrooms and fry them in the butter for 5 minutes until tender. Mix together the cornflour or arrowroot and cream; add this to the mushrooms and stir over the heat briefly until slightly thickened. Season with salt, pepper and nutmeg. Keep the mixture warm, but don't let it boil.

Have ready a large piece of greaseproof paper dusted with Parmesan cheese and turn the roulade out on to this; strip off the silicon paper. Spread the filling over the roulade, then roll it up like a swiss roll and slide it on to a warmed serving dish. Return to the oven for 5 minutes to heat through, then serve immediately.

SPICED VEGETABLES
WITH DHAL SAUCE

This is a lovely dish, not hot but lightly spiced. The dhal sauce supplies the protein and it's nice served with spiced rice, page 112, poppadums, mango chutney and the banana, peanut and spring onion salad on page 81.

Serves 4

3 tablespoons oil
1 onion, peeled and chopped
1 large clove garlic, peeled and crushed
1 teaspoon turmeric
1 teaspoon ground coriander
1 teaspoon ground cumin
1 bay leaf

2 carrots, about 225g (8 oz) in all, scraped and thinly sliced
450g (1 lb) potatoes, peeled and cubed
2 leeks, washed and sliced
150ml (¼ pint) water
sea salt and freshly ground black pepper

For the dhal sauce

1 onion, peeled and chopped
1 clove garlic, peeled and
   crushed
1 tablespoon oil
125g (4 oz) split red lentils

1 teaspoon ground coriander
1 teaspoon cumin
550ml (1 pint) stock *or* water
1 bay leaf

Heat the oil in a fairly large saucepan and fry the onion for 5 minutes, then add the garlic, spices and bay leaf and stir over the heat for 1–2 minutes. Put in the remaining vegetables and stir over the heat for a further 1–2 minutes so that they are all coated with the oil and spices. Add the water and a little salt and pepper. Cover and leave to simmer for 15–20 minutes, until the vegetables are all tender, stirring from time to time and checking towards the end to make sure they do not burn dry – there will be very little water left. Alternatively, the spiced vegetables can be put into an ovenproof casserole and baked at 160°C (325°F), gas mark 3, for about 1–1½ hours, until tender when pierced with the point of a knife.

To make the sauce, first fry the onion and garlic in the oil for 5 minutes, until beginning to soften, then stir in the lentils and spices and cook for a further minute or two. Add the stock or water and bay leaf; bring up to the boil, then leave to simmer gently for 15–20 minutes, until the lentils are tender and pale gold in colour. Remove the bay leaf, liquidize the sauce and add salt and pepper to taste.

Serve the vegetables with the sauce.

Loaves, Bakes and Burgers

Although a nut or lentil loaf takes a little effort to prepare, this is more than justified by the fact that, like a joint of meat, it can be served twice, first hot then cold, which saves time in the end.

I think a savoury loaf needs something moist to go with it; a light puréed vegetable or a sauce such as mushroom and soured cream (page 161) or fresh tomato (page 162). A chilled yoghurt and herb dressing or mayonnaise goes well with cold sliced nut or lentil loaf and, sliced thinly, these are also good as fillings for sandwiches or rolls.

The burgers are also good inside fresh light rolls or French bread, especially if they're cooked and eaten sizzling hot out of doors, with plenty of good mustard and salad to go with them.

All the nut loaves freeze well, either before or after baking, though I think part-baking them for about thirty minutes before freezing gives the best results. The burgers are best frozen uncovered on a baking sheet then packed in a polythene bag. You can cook these from frozen.

CHESTNUT, SAGE AND RED WINE LOAF

This is a moist savoury loaf which slices well either hot or cold. Served with baked red cabbage and jacket potatoes and soured cream it makes a very pleasant winter meal; it's also very good as a vegetarian alternative to Christmas turkey, with a wine sauce, bread sauce, roast potatoes and baby sprouts.

Serves 6

butter and dried breadcrumbs
  for lining loaf tin
350g (12 oz) dried chestnuts *or* 1
  kilo (2¹/₄ lb) fresh chestnuts
50g (2 oz) butter *or*
  polyunsaturated margarine
1 large onion, peeled and
  chopped
2 celery stalks, finely chopped
2 garlic cloves, peeled and
  crushed

2 tablespoons chopped fresh
  sage *or* 1 teaspoon dried
1 tablespoon red wine
1 egg
sea salt and freshly ground black
  pepper
1 fresh sage leaf if available, to
  garnish

Set the oven to 180°C (350°F), gas mark 4. Prepare a 450g (1 lb) loaf tin by lining the base and narrow sides with a long strip of silicon paper; brush well with butter and sprinkle lightly with the dried breadcrumbs.

If you're using dried chestnuts, cover with boiling water then leave to soak for at least 2 hours; simmer in plenty of water for about 1¹/₂ hours until tender. For fresh chestnuts, nick each with a knife then simmer in plenty of water for about 10 minutes until the cuts open. Take the chestnuts from the water one by one and strip off the skins with a sharp, pointed knife. Put the skinned chestnuts into a saucepan, cover with water and simmer for 20–30 minutes until tender. Drain and mash the chestnuts. Melt the butter or margarine in a large saucepan and fry the onion and celery for 10 minutes, without browning. Add the chestnuts, garlic, sage, wine and egg and mix together, seasoning with salt and pepper.

Lay the sage leaf, if using, in the base of the prepared loaf tin and spoon the chestnut mixture on top, smooth over the surface and cover with a piece of foil. Bake the loaf in the pre-heated oven for 1 hour. To serve, slip a knife round the sides of the loaf and turn out on to a warm dish.

LENTIL AND CIDER LOAF

The cider gives this loaf a lovely rich fruity flavour, though you could leave it out and use a good vegetable stock if you prefer, or try a cheapish red wine instead which is also delicious and better if you want to drink red wine with the meal. The loaf is rich in protein and very good hot, perhaps with fresh tomato sauce and lemon potatoes; or cold, with salad and home-made mayonnaise. It can also be used as a sandwich filling, cut in thin slices and spread with mild mustard or chutney.

Serves 6–8

175g (6 oz) split red lentils
400ml (³/4 pint) cider
butter and dried breadcrumbs
  for lining loaf tin
1 large onion, peeled and
  chopped
1 carrot, about 50g (2 oz),
  scraped and chopped
1 stick of celery, chopped
1 garlic clove, peeled and
  crushed
25g (1 oz) butter
1 teaspoon dried thyme

50g (2 oz) hazel nuts, roasted for
  about 20 minutes in a
  moderate oven until nuts are
  golden beneath the skins, then
  ground in a liquidizer
50g (2 oz) cheese, grated
1 tablespoon fresh parsley,
  chopped
1 egg
sea salt and freshly ground black
  pepper
parsley sprigs to decorate

Put the lentils and cider into a saucepan and bring to the boil; turn the heat down, half-cover the saucepan and leave to simmer over a fairly low heat for 20 minutes, until the lentils are tender and all the water absorbed.

When the lentils are nearly cooked, set the oven to 180°C (350°F), gas mark 4. Prepare a 450g (1 lb) loaf tin by lining the base and narrow sides with a long strip of silicon paper; brush well with butter and sprinkle lightly with dried breadcrumbs. Next, fry the onion, carrot, celery and garlic in the butter for 10 minutes, until they are softened and lightly browned. Add the fried vegetables to the lentils, together with the thyme, nuts, cheese, parsley and egg. Mix everything together thoroughly and add salt and plenty of pepper to taste.

Spoon the mixture into the prepared tin, smooth over the surface and cover with a piece of foil. Bake the loaf in the pre-heated oven for 1 hour, then remove the foil and cook for a further 10–15 minutes, uncovered if necessary, to brown the top. To serve, slip a knife round the sides of the loaf and turn out on to a warm dish. Decorate the top with some sprigs of fresh green parsley.

PINE NUTMEAT WITH HERB STUFFING

This dish consists of two layers of moist, delicately-flavoured, white nutmeat with a layer of green herb stuffing in the middle. It's a favourite vegetarian alternative to Christmas turkey and popular with my family at any time. The pine nuts are expensive and, though lovely for a special occasion, can be replaced by cheaper white nuts such as cashews or ground almonds. I would serve this loaf with golden roast potatoes and either wine sauce and a lightly-cooked green vegetable or a purée of Brussels sprouts; the cranberry and apple sauce also goes very well with it.

Serves 6

butter and dried breadcrumbs
   for lining loaf tin
25g (1 oz) butter
1 onion, peeled and chopped
225g (8 oz) pine nuts *or* a
   mixture of pine nuts, ground
   almonds and cashew nuts,
   grated

4 tablespoons milk
125g (4 oz) soft, white
   breadcrumbs
2 eggs
sea salt and freshly ground black
   pepper
grated nutmeg

For the stuffing

175g (6 oz) soft breadcrumbs,
  white *or* brown
125g (4 oz) butter
grated rind and juice of ¹/₂ small
  lemon
¹/₂ teaspoon dried marjoram

¹/₂ teaspoon dried thyme
4 heaped tablespoons fresh
  parsley, chopped
sea salt and freshly ground black
  pepper

To finish

2 tablespoons pine nuts, lightly
  roasted

parsley sprigs
lemon slices

Set the oven to 180°C (350°F), gas mark 4. Line a 450g (1 lb) loaf
tin with a long strip of silicon paper to cover the narrow sides
and base of the tin; grease very well with butter and sprinkle
with dried breadcrumbs – this helps the loaf to come out of the
tin cleanly. Melt the butter in a medium-sized saucepan and fry
the onion for 10 minutes until soft but not browned. Take the
saucepan off the heat and mix in the rest of the ingredients,
seasoning well with salt, pepper and grated nutmeg. Next make
the stuffing by mixing all the ingredients together and seasoning
well.

To assemble the loaf, first spoon half the nut mixture into the
prepared tin, then, with your hands, press the stuffing mixture
into a rectangle which is the right size to make a layer on top
of the nut mixture; put it gently in place and spoon the rest of
the nut mixture on top. Smooth the surface, cover with a piece
of buttered foil and bake for 1 hour. After this, remove the foil
and have a look at the nutmeat; if you think it needs to be a bit
browner on top, pop it back into the oven, uncovered, for a
further 5–10 minutes. If possible, leave the loaf for 3–4 minutes
after you take it out of the oven – this helps it to 'settle' and
come out of the tin more easily – then slip a knife down the sides
of the loaf, turn it out of the tin on to a warmed serving dish
and strip off the piece of silicon paper. Garnish with the roasted
nuts, parsley and lemon.

WHITE NUTMEAT WITH CAPERS

My original idea with this nutmeat was to use green pepper-corns; when it was sliced I wanted to get the effect of white flecked with green. But the number of peppercorns needed to get that effect made the loaf far too hot! So then I hit on the idea of using capers instead and I must say I was very pleased with the result: the slices look just as I envisaged them and the capers give the loaf a lovely tangy flavour. The loaf is good served hot with a rich sauce – Béarnaise is lovely – or cold, with mayonnaise and salad.

Serves 6

butter and dried breadcrumbs
  for lining loaf tin
25g (1 oz) butter
1 onion, peeled and chopped
225g (8 oz) cashew nuts, grated,
  or half cashew nuts and half
  ground almonds

4 tablespoons milk
125g (4 oz) soft white
  breadcrumbs
2 eggs
sea salt and freshly ground black
  pepper
75g (3 oz) capers

To finish

a few extra capers
whole cashew nuts, lightly roasted

Set the oven to 180°C (350°F), gas mark 4. Line a 450g (1 lb) loaf tin with a long strip of silicon paper to cover the narrow sides and base of the tin; grease very well with butter and sprinkle with dried breadcrumbs – this helps the loaf to come out of the tin cleanly. Melt the butter in a medium-sized saucepan and fry the onion for 10 minutes until soft but not browned. Take the saucepan off the heat and mix in the nuts, milk, breadcrumbs, egg and a good seasoning of salt and pepper. Lastly, carefully fold in the capers, being careful not to mash them.

Spoon the mixture into the prepared tin, smooth the surface, cover with a piece of buttered foil and bake for 1 hour. After this, remove the foil and have a look at the nutmeat; if you think it needs to be a bit browner on top, pop it back into the oven, uncovered, for a further 5–10 minutes. If possible, leave the loaf for 3–4 minutes after you take it out of the oven – this helps it to 'settle' and come out of the tin more easily – then slip a knife down the sides of the loaf, turn it out of the tin on to a warmed serving dish and strip off the piece of silicon paper. Decorate with a row of capers down the centre and some roasted cashew nuts either side.

LENTIL AND MUSHROOM BURGERS

The mushrooms make these burgers moist while the lentils add texture and protein. The burgers hold together well and can be cooked in the oven on an oiled baking sheet, fried on top of the stove or grilled over a barbecue. I like them with a dollop of creamy Béarnaise sauce – or mayonnaise – and fresh watercress; but they are also lovely when eaten in a soft roll with lots of mustard or chutney.

Serves 4

15g (¹/2 oz) butter
1 tablespoon oil
1 onion, peeled and chopped
450g (1 lb) mushrooms, washed and chopped
2 large garlic cloves, peeled and crushed
125g (4 oz) (dry weight) continental lentils, cooked and very well drained

2 tablespoons fresh parsley, chopped
sea salt and freshly ground black pepper
flour for coating
oil for shallow-frying – optional

If you're going to bake the burgers in the oven, set it to 200°C (400°F), gas mark 6. Heat the butter and oil in a large saucepan and fry the onion for 5 minutes, until beginning to soften, then put in the mushrooms and garlic. Fry over a moderate heat for 20–25 minutes, until all the liquid has evaporated and the mushrooms are reduced to a thick purée. Stir them from time to time while they are cooking. Then take the saucepan off the heat and mix in all the other ingredients, seasoning to taste with salt and pepper. Form the mixture into burger shapes and roll the burgers lightly in flour. Place them on a greased baking sheet and bake for about 30 minutes, turning them over half way through the cooking time. Alternatively, fry the burgers quickly in a little hot oil, or brush them with oil and grill on both sides.

WHITE NUT RISSOLES
BAKED WITH MUSHROOMS

In this recipe, light, delicately flavoured nut rissoles are baked on a moist base of fried button mushrooms and onions. It's delicious with a light vegetable dish or fluffy brown rice and a green salad.

Serves 3–4

For the sauce

.15g (¹/2 oz) butter
1 tablespoon oil
1 large onion, peeled and
  chopped
2 garlic cloves, peeled and
  crushed

225g (8 oz) button mushrooms,
  washed and sliced
2 tablespoons white wine *or*
  cider
2 tablespoons single cream –
  optional

For the nut rissoles

125g (4 oz) cashew nuts, grated
50g (2 oz) soft white
  breadcrumbs
50g (2 oz) white cheese, finely
  grated

1 egg
¹/2 teaspoon dried thyme
sea salt and freshly ground black
  pepper
fresh parsley, chopped

First prepare the mushroom mixture. Heat the butter and oil in a medium-sized saucepan and fry the onion for 5 minutes, until beginning to soften, then add the garlic and mushrooms and fry for a further 5 minutes. Add the wine or cider, let the mixture bubble and scrape down the crusty bits from the sides of the pan. Remove from the heat and season to taste. Pour the mixture into a shallow casserole dish.

Set the oven to 180°C (350°F), gas mark 4. Make the rissoles by mixing all the ingredients together; season with salt and plenty of pepper. Form the mixture into eight rissoles and put them on top of the mushroom mixture. Bake, uncovered, for 25–30 minutes, until the rissoles are puffed up a little and firm but not hard. Pour the cream into the casserole dish, around the rissoles, sprinkle with chopped parsley and serve.

A pleasant variation is to put a cooked chestnut (or a well-drained canned chestnut) into the centre of each nut rissole, moulding the white nut mixture gently round it.

BROWN NUT RISSOLES IN TOMATO SAUCE

This is really a variation of the above recipe except that, by using brown nuts and breadcrumbs for the rissoles and baking them in a fresh-tasting tomato sauce, you get quite a different effect. These are delicious served with buttery wholewheat spaghetti, Parmesan cheese and a crisp green salad with a good olive oil dressing.

Serves 3–4

For the sauce

1 tablespoon oil
1 onion, peeled and chopped
1 garlic clove, peeled and
  crushed
450g (1 lb) tomatoes, peeled and
  chopped, *or* use a 425g (15 oz)
  can

sea salt and freshly ground black
  pepper

For the nut rissoles

1 small onion, fried
125g (4 oz) brown nuts such as
  unblanched almonds *or*
  roasted hazel nuts – see page
  36
50g (2 oz) soft wholewheat
  breadcrumbs
50g (2 oz) vegetarian Cheddar
  cheese, finely grated

2 heaped teaspoons tomato
  purée
1 egg
$1/2$ teaspoon dried thyme
sea salt and freshly ground black
  pepper

Start by making the sauce. Heat the oil in a medium-sized saucepan and fry the onion for 10 minutes, until softened but not browned. Add the garlic and tomatoes, and cook for a further 15 minutes, until the tomatoes have collapsed and reduced to a purée. Sieve or liquidize the mixture and season with salt and pepper.

Next, set the oven to 180°C (350°F), gas mark 4, and make the rissoles by simply mixing all the ingredients together and seasoning to taste. Form the mixture into eight rissoles and place them in a greased, shallow, ovenproof dish. Pour the sauce over the rissoles and bake them in the pre-heated oven for 25–30 minutes, until they are puffy but firm to the touch.

NUT RISSOLES IN RATATOUILLE

Another variation is to bake the nut rissoles, either the white or brown version, in ratatouille. Prepare and cook the ratatouille, as described on page 110, and put it into a shallow ovenproof dish; put the nut rissoles on top of the ratatouille and bake as described for nut rissoles in tomato sauce, page 133. These go well with fluffy brown rice and a green salad, and, if you use canned ratatouille, perhaps enlivened with a dash of wine or cider, this makes a good emergency dish.

Pies, Pastries and Pizzas

Flans, pizzas and pies are so useful, being substantial yet easy to eat and versatile enough to be eaten hot or cold, on their own or as part of a meal, with sauces and hot vegetables, or salads.

If they are made with wholewheat flour they are also healthy and nutritious, useful for everyday cooking as well as special occasions though, as they're fairly high in fat, it's a good idea to serve them with fairly plainly cooked vegetables or salads without too much oil, with a fresh fruit pudding.

Again for health reasons, I like to use polyunsaturated margarine where I can in cooking, and I do find you can make a very good, light, wholewheat shortcrust pastry with it. I use that for most flans and pies, but the flaky pastry which I like to make as a treat for special occasions does need a hard fat and for this I use a block of well-chilled butter.

ASPARAGUS FLAN

This is a creamy, delicious flan with a crisp pastry case. You could use all cream, if you like, but I find this lighter, half-and-half mixture of cream and *fromage blanc* works well. This is lovely for an early summer lunch, with buttered new potatoes.

Serves 6

For the pastry

175g (6 oz) plain wholewheat
flour
75g (3 oz) polyunsaturated
margarine *or* butter

1¹/₂ tablespoons water

For the filling

450g (1 lb) fresh *or* frozen
asparagus
sea salt and freshly ground black
pepper
2 tablespoons oil
1 small onion, peeled and
chopped

125g (4 oz) Cheddar cheese,
grated
150ml (¹/₄ pint) single cream
125g (4 oz) *fromage blanc*
2 eggs
fresh parsley, chopped

First cook the asparagus for the filling. If you're using fresh asparagus, break off the hard stems at the base – these ends are too tough to eat but can be used to make a stock for asparagus soup. Wash the asparagus gently to remove any grit, then place it in a steamer and cook for about 10 minutes: it should be just tender when pierced with a pointed knife. Cook frozen asparagus according to the directions on the packet. Drain asparagus and season with salt and pepper.

To make the pastry, sift the flour into a large bowl, and just tip in the bran which will be left in the sieve. Rub the fat into the flour, using your fingertips or a fork, until the mixture resembles fine breadcrumbs – if the fat is soft you might find it easiest to start this process with a fork – then add the cold water and press the mixture together to form a dough. If there's time leave this dough to rest for 30 minutes (this makes it easier to roll out but isn't essential). Set the oven to 200°C (400°F), gas mark 6, and if possible place a heavy baking sheet on the top shelf to heat up with the oven. Roll out the pastry and ease it into an 20cm (8 in) flan tin which has been lightly greased. Trim the edges and prick the base. Put the flan case into the oven on top of the baking sheet and bake for 15 minutes, until the pastry is lightly browned and the base feels set and crisp to touch.

While the flan case is in the oven, heat the 2 tablespoons of oil in a large saucepan and fry the onion for 10 minutes, until the onion has softened and browned lightly. Have the fried onion piping hot when you take the flan out of the oven and pour this, oil and all, over the base of the hot flan case, making sure that the oil spreads over the whole of the base. This makes the pastry crisp (and ensures that it will stay crisp after the filling is added) but you must put the hot oil and onion into the flan case as soon as it comes out of the oven. After that the flan case can be cooled and the rest of the filling added later if more convenient.

To finish the flan, reduce the oven setting to 180°C (350°F), gas mark 4. Arrange the cooked asparagus in the base of the flan and sprinkle with half the cheese. Whisk the cream, *fromage blanc* and eggs together until smooth; season with salt and freshly ground black pepper. Pour this mixture over the asparagus and cheese and sprinkle with the remaining cheese. Bake the flan for 30 minutes, until the filling is puffed up, golden and set. Sprinkle with chopped parsley before serving.

AUBERGINE, RED PEPPER AND CHEESE FLAN

This is a pretty flan with a chunky, aubergine filling set in a light custard. I think the nutty flavour of the wholewheat pastry goes well with the onion and aubergine filling. This flan is best served hot, with buttered new potatoes and French beans.

Serves 6

For the pastry

175g (6 oz) plain wholewheat
  flour
75g (3 oz) polyunsaturated
  margarine *or* butter

1½ tablespoons water

For the filling

1 medium-sized aubergine, about
  225g (8 oz)
3 tablespoons oil
2 large onions, peeled and
  chopped
1 red pepper, about 175g (6 oz)
1 fat clove of garlic, peeled and
  crushed in a little salt

sea salt and freshly ground black
  pepper
125g (4 oz) Cheddar cheese,
  grated
2 eggs
150ml (¼ pint) milk

First make a start on the filling by preparing the aubergine.
Wash the aubergine and remove the stem, then cut the
aubergine down into 1cm (½ in) cubes. Put these into a
colander, sprinkle them with salt and then place a plate and a
weight on top and leave for at least 30 minutes. After that rinse
the pieces of aubergine under the cold tap and squeeze them to
remove excess water.

Set the oven to 200°C (400°F), gas mark 6. Make the pastry
flan case as described for the asparagus flan, page 136, and bake
for 15 minutes.

While the flan case is in the oven, heat 2 tablespoons of the
oil in a large saucepan and fry the onion for 10 minutes until the
onion has softened and browned lightly. Have the fried onion
piping hot when you take the flan out of the oven and pour this,
oil and all, over the base of the hot flan case, making sure that
the oil spreads over the whole of the base.

To finish the flan, reduce the oven setting to 180°C (350°F),
gas mark 4. Heat the remaining tablespoon of oil in a
medium-sized saucepan and fry the aubergine, red pepper and
garlic for about 10 minutes, until they are tender but not too
soft. Season with salt and freshly ground black pepper. Put two
thirds of the grated cheese in the base of the flan case, then
spoon the aubergine mixture on top and sprinkle with the rest
of the cheese. Whisk together the eggs and milk and pour evenly
over the top of the flan. Bake towards the top of the oven for
50–60 minutes, until the filling is set and golden.

CAULIFLOWER, STILTON AND WALNUT FLAN

This flan consists of a crisp wholewheat pastry base with a filling of cauliflower with Stilton cheese and walnuts. Serve with a crisp salad, and new potatoes with parsley for a more substantial meal.

Serves 6

For the pastry

175g (6 oz) plain wholewheat flour

75g (3 oz) polyunsaturated margarine *or* butter

1^1/2 tablespoons water

For the filling

1 medium-sized cauliflower – about 450g (1 lb) when trimmed

sea salt and freshly ground black pepper

125g (4 oz) Stilton cheese, preferably white, as it gives the dish a better colour, grated *or* crumbled

75g (3 oz) walnuts, coarsely chopped

2 eggs

150ml (^{1}/4 pint) milk

Set the oven to 200°C (400°F), gas mark 6. Make the pastry flan case as described for the asparagus flan, page 136, and bake for 15 minutes. Turn the oven setting down to 190°C (375°F), gas mark 5.

While the flan case is cooking, make the filling. Break the cauliflower into florets, then slice these so that they will lie fairly flat in the flan case later. Cook the cauliflower in 2.5cm (1 in) fast-boiling lightly salted water for 5 minutes until just barely tender when pierced with the point of a knife. Drain very well and season with salt and pepper.

Put two thirds of the cheese and half the walnuts in the base of the flan case, then put in the cauliflower, arranging it so that it's just about level with the top of the flan case and sprinkle with the rest of the cheese and walnuts. Whisk together the eggs and milk and pour evenly over the top of the flan. Bake towards the top of the oven for 50–60 minutes, until the filling is set. Serve at once if possible.

DEEP DISH MUSHROOM PIE

My aim with this was to make a pie which could be cut into slices for a party or buffet, as you might cut up a long meat pie. It looks very attractive, especially if you can make it in a long, thin loaf tin. I have one with collapsible sides which is 7.5cm (3 in) deep with an inside base measurement of 25 × 8cm (9³/₄ × 3¹/₄ in) and a top measurement of 27.5 × 10.5cm (10³/₄ × 4¹/₄ in), and that is ideal, but the capacity is the same as that of a standard 900g (2 lb) loaf tin, so you could use that instead, lined with greased foil to help ease the pie out after baking.

Serves 10

For the pastry

350g (12 oz) wholewheat flour
salt
225g (8 oz) polyunsaturated
  margarine

beaten egg to glaze

For the filling

25g (1 oz) butter
1 large onion, peeled and
  chopped
2 large garlic cloves, peeled and
  crushed
350g (12 oz) button mushrooms,
  wiped
275g (10 oz) ground almonds
125g (4 oz) cheese, grated
2 eggs, beaten
1 tablespoon lemon juice

3 tablespoons fresh parsley,
  chopped
1 teaspoon ground mace
freshly ground black pepper
3 or 4 hardboiled eggs –
  optional: these go down the
  centre of the loaf and the
  number needed depends on
  the length of both the tin and
  the eggs, so try them first

140

First make the pastry. Sift the flour into a large bowl with a little salt, and just tip in the bran which will be left in the sieve. Rub the fat into the flour – a fork is easiest for this – then press the mixture together to form a dough. If there's time leave this dough to rest for 30 minutes (this makes it easier to roll out but isn't essential).

Meanwhile make the filling. Melt the butter in a large saucepan and fry the onion for 10 minutes until soft but not browned; add the garlic and fry for a further minute or two. Then take the saucepan off the heat and stir in all the remaining ingredients except the hardboiled eggs. Season with salt and pepper.

Set the oven to 200°C (400°F), gas mark 6, and if possible place a heavy baking sheet on the top shelf to heat up with the oven. Roll out three quarters of the pastry and ease it into the loaf tin which has been well greased if it's a collapsible one or lined with well-greased foil if not. This is not an easy process as the pastry is fragile, and I find it usually breaks and has to go in in several separate pieces – this doesn't matter; just patch it up and press it together. Spoon in half the filling, then put the hardboiled eggs on top of this, if you're using them, and cover with the remaining mixture. Roll the last piece of pastry into a rectangle to fit the top of the pie and press into position. Neaten and trim the edges, decorate with the pastry trimmings, brush with beaten egg and make several holes in the top to allow the steam to escape.

Bake the pie for 30 minutes in the pre-heated oven, then turn the oven setting down to 180°C (350°F), gas mark 4, and bake for a further 30 minutes. Leave the pie to cool in the tin, then remove it carefully. It slices best when chilled a little.

DEEP DISH STRIPY VEGETABLE PIE

This idea came to me when I was telling a friend about the deep dish mushroom pie, above, and she said why didn't I try a variation of a Cornish pasty, as these, traditionally, are made from root vegetables and do not contain meat. So I used the same deep tin and, so that the pie would look good when sliced, I put the thinly-sliced vegetables into the tin in layers. I was very pleased with the result; the pie looks good and slices well. Other variations are possible; you can add some thin layers of different coloured grated cheeses or some chopped parsley to give a green layer. It's delicious served hot, with some yoghurt and spring onion sauce or lemon mayonnaise.

Serves 10

For the pastry

350g (12 oz) wholewheat flour   beaten egg to glaze
salt
225g (8 oz) polyunsaturated
  margarine

For the filling

225g (8 oz) swede *or* parsnip,   freshly ground black pepper
  peeled   grated nutmeg
450g (1 lb) carrots, scraped
225g (8 oz) potatoes *or* turnips,
  peeled

First make the pastry as described for the deep dish mushroom pie, page 141, and leave it to chill while you prepare the filling.

To do this, slice the vegetables as thinly as possible, preferably on an electric grater or food processor. Keep the different types separate, covered with water if necessary, until you're ready to use them.

Set the oven to 200°C (400°F), gas mark 6. Roll out the pastry and line the loaf tin as described for the deep dish mushroom pie. Put the sliced swede or parsnip in an even layer in the base of the pie, pressing it down well. Season well with salt, pepper and grated nutmeg. Follow this with a layer of half the carrot, then the potato or turnip, followed by the rest of the carrot, seasoning each layer. Roll the last piece of pastry into a rectangle to fit the top of the pie and press into position. Neaten and trim the edges, decorate with the pastry trimmings, brush with beaten egg and make several holes in the top to allow the steam to escape. Bake the pie for 30 minutes in the pre-heated oven, then turn the oven setting down to 160°C (325°F), gas mark 3, and bake for a further hour, covering the pastry with foil for the last half hour or so if it is getting too brown. Remove the pie from the tin and serve hot; or, if you are going to serve it cold, let it cool in the tin, then remove it carefully. I like it best hot.

FLAKY MUSHROOM ROLL

This is a lovely flaky golden pastry roll with a moist mushroom filling. The pastry isn't difficult to make but you need to allow time for it to chill in the fridge before use.

Serves 6

For the pastry

225g (8 oz) hard butter, taken from the fridge
150ml (¼ pint) ice-cold water
tiny squeeze lemon juice

225g (8 oz) plain 81 per cent wholewheat flour
beaten egg, to glaze

For the filling

25g (1 oz) butter
1 onion, peeled and chopped
1 large clove garlic, peeled and crushed
450g (1 lb) mushrooms, wiped and chopped
2 heaped tablespoons fresh parsley, chopped

2 hardboiled eggs, chopped – optional
350g (12 oz) cooked brown rice – this is about 125g (4 oz) dry weight
½ teaspoon powdered mace
sea salt and freshly ground black pepper

First make the pastry. Make sure that the butter is really hard and the water as cold as possible: I usually put both in the fridge for an hour or so before making the pastry. It's a good idea to put the flour into a large bowl and chill that, too, if you can.

Cut the butter into 6mm ($^1/_4$ in) dice and put them into the bowl with the flour. Mix lightly so that the butter gets dusted with the flour, then add the water and lemon juice and mix gently with a metal spoon to make a loose, lumpy dough.

Put the dough on to a well-floured board and turn it once or twice in the flour. Then, using light strokes, roll it out into a long oblong. Fold the top third of the oblong down and the bottom third up so that you have three layers. Half turn the block of pastry to the right, so that the folded edges are at the side. Roll, fold and turn the pastry again, doing this four times inall. Put the fold of dough into a polythene bag and chill it in the fridge for at least two hours before using it.

To assemble and finish the roll, set the oven to 220°C (425°F), gas mark 7. Sprinkle a little flour on a pastry board and roll the fold of pastry into a square about 30 x 30 cm (12 x 12 in). Put the mushroom mixture in a heap in the centre of the pastry and wrap the pastry over it, moistening the edges with a little cold water and pressing them together to make a neat oblong. Place this, seam-side down, on a baking sheet; roll out the pastry trimmings and cut out some leaves to garnish the roll, then make one or two cuts or holes in the top to allow the steam to escape, brush with beaten egg and bake at the top of the oven for 30 minutes, then turn the heat down to 190°C (375°F), gas mark 5, for a further 25–30 minutes. For the filling, fry the onion, garlic and mushrooms in the butter for 10 minutes, then simply add the remaining ingredients and season to taste. This is nice with the yoghurt and fresh herb sauce (page 162), made with some fennel if available, and a green salad.

MUSHROOM PUDDING

This is a steamed pudding, rather like a vegetarian steak and kidney pudding. It's very easy to do and makes a warming meal in winter. I like to serve it with mashed potatoes and the red cabbage bake on page 100.

Serves 4

For the pastry

175g (6 oz) plain wholewheat
  flour
75g (3 oz) polyunsaturated
  margarine

125g (4 oz) cheese, grated
2 tablespoons water

For the filling

350g (12 oz) dark mushrooms,
  wiped and sliced
1 onion, peeled and chopped
1 teaspoon tomato purée
1 small garlic clove, peeled and
  crushed

sea salt and freshly ground black
  pepper
1 teaspoon yeast extract
2 tablespoons hot water

First make the pastry. Sift the flour into a large bowl, and just tip in the bran which will be left in the sieve. Rub the fat into the flour using your fingertips or a fork until the mixture resembles fine breadcrumbs – if the fat is soft you might find it easiest to start this process with a fork – then add the cheese and water and press the mixture together to form a dough. If there's time leave this dough to rest for 30 minutes (this makes it easier to roll out but isn't essential). Grease an 850ml (1½ pint) pudding basin.

To make the filling, put the mushrooms into a bowl and mix with the remaining ingredients, softening the yeast extract in the hot water. Roll out two thirds of the pastry and use to line the pudding basin; spoon the mushroom mixture into this, then cover with the rest of the pastry, rolled out to fit the top. Trim edges and prick the top with a fork. Cover with a piece of foil, secured with string. Steam the pudding for 2½ hours (or 1 hour in a pressure cooker). When it's done, slip a knife down the sides of the bowl to loosen the pudding, then turn out onto a warmed serving dish.

WALNUT PÂTÉ EN CROÛTE

This makes a delicious main course for a special meal: a moist wine-flavoured pâté in a crisp crust of golden pastry. The quantities I've given here make a handsome dish that will feed 12 easily. If you think this is too much, the amounts can simply be halved; but the pâté is also delicious cold and will freeze well before cooking. As for the flaky mushroom roll, remember to chill before use: I try to make it the night before I need it, if possible.

Serves 12

For the flaky pastry

225g (8 oz) hard butter, taken
 from the fridge
150ml (¹/4 pint) ice-cold water

tiny squeeze lemon juice
225g (8 oz) plain 81 per cent
 wholewheat flour

For the nutmeat pâté

25g (1 oz) butter
1 large onion, peeled and
 chopped
1 stick of celery, finely chopped
2 large garlic cloves, peeled and
 crushed
125g (4 oz) walnuts, grated
350g (12 oz) cashew nuts, grated
225g (8 oz) chestnut purée
125g (4 oz) Cheddar cheese,
 grated

2 eggs
2 tablespoons brandy
¹/2 teaspoon paprika
¹/2 teaspoon dried thyme
sea salt and freshly ground black
 pepper
225g (8 oz) baby button
 mushrooms, washed
beaten egg to glaze

First make the pastry as described for the flaky mushroom roll on page 143 – you need to do this an hour or so in advance to give it a chance to chill before you use it.

While the pastry is chilling, make the nutmeat pâté. Melt the butter in a medium-sized saucepan and fry the onion and celery for 10 minutes, until soft but not browned. Remove from the heat and stir in the garlic, nuts, cheese, eggs, brandy, paprika, thyme and plenty of seasoning to taste.

To assemble and finish the pâté, set the oven to 220°C (425°F), gas mark 7. Sprinkle a little flour on a pastry board and roll the fold of pastry into a rectangle about 30 x 40cm (12 x 16 in). Put the pâté in the centre of the pastry and place the mushrooms on top. Brush the edges of the pastry with a little cold water, then fold them over to encase the pâté and mushrooms completely but not too tightly, to allow for the pâté to expand a little as it cooks. Place the pastry parcel seam-side down on a baking sheet; roll out the pastry trimmings and cut out some leaves to garnish the roll, then make one or two cuts or holes in the top to allow the steam to escape. Brush with beaten egg and bake at the top of the oven for 30 minutes, then turn the heat down to 190°C (375°F), gas mark 5, for a further 25–30 minutes. I like to serve this with a purée of Brussels sprouts and new potatoes with butter and chopped parsley; the mushroom sauce and soured cream on page 161 also goes well with it.

SPECIAL PIZZA

A pizza isn't nearly as difficult to make as many people think and it's one of the most delicious vegetarian dishes. This recipe takes about 2½ hours to make from start to finish, but during most of that time the dough is rising, and you're not tied to the kitchen.

Serves 4–8: makes four 20cm (8 in) or two 30cm (12 in) pizzas

For the base

25g (1 oz) fresh yeast *or*
   1 tablespoon dried yeast and
   1 teaspoon sugar
200ml (7 fl oz) warm water
400g (14 oz) wholewheat flour

2 teaspoons salt
25g (1 oz) soft butter *or*
   vegetable margarine
1 large egg, beaten

For the topping

2 tablespoons olive oil
2 large onions, peeled and chopped
1 garlic clove, crushed
125g (4 oz) button mushrooms, wiped and sliced
2 350g (12 oz) cans tomatoes, very well drained
sea salt and freshly ground black pepper
4–6 canned artichoke hearts, sliced

185g ($6^1/2$ oz) canned red peppers, drained and cut into slices
225g (8 oz) white cheese – I use vegetarian Cheshire, cut into thin slices
a few black olives
2 teaspoons oregano
olive oil

If you're using fresh yeast, crumble it into a small bowl and gradually blend in the water with a spoon. For dried yeast, put the water into a bowl, stir in the sugar and then sprinkle in the yeast; stir once. Leave on one side for 10 minutes until the yeast has frothed up with a head, like a glass of beer.

Put the flour and salt into a large bowl and rub in the butter or margarine with your fingertips. Make a well in the centre and pour in the yeast mixture and the beaten egg. Mix to a firm dough which will leave the sides of the bowl clean – add a tiny bit more flour or water if necessary to achieve this. Turn the dough out onto a clean working surface and knead for 10 minutes, until the texture becomes smooth and pliable. Then put the dough back into the mixing bowl, cover the bowl with a piece of clingfilm and leave until the dough has doubled in size: this takes $1^1/2$ hours at room temperature.

Set the oven to 200°C (400°F), gas mark 6. Take the dough out of the bowl and press it firmly all over with your knuckles to 'knock it back' and remove any large pockets of air. Knead for 2 minutes, then divide the dough into two or four pieces and roll each into a 30cm (12 in) or 20cm (8 in) circle. These can be put onto large ovenproof pizza plates or into well-greased flan tins or oven sheets, whichever is most convenient.

It's best to make the filling while the dough is rising for the first time. Heat the oil in a medium-sized saucepan and fry the onion and garlic for 10 minutes, until softened, then add the mushrooms and cook for a further 2–3 minutes. Remove from the heat, stir in the tomatoes chopping them up with a spoon and season to taste.

Spoon the tomato mixture on top of the pizzas, dividing it evenly between them. Arrange the artichoke hearts, red pepper strips, slices of cheese and olives on top; sprinkle with oregano and a little olive oil. Leave pizzas for 15–20 minutes until the dough is slightly puffy, then bake for about 20 minutes, until the topping is bubbling and golden and the bread puffed up and lightly browned. Serve at once, with a good green salad and some red wine or chilled cider.

INDIVIDUAL PIZZAS

I find it very handy to have some small pizzas in the deep freeze, ready to be heated up quickly from frozen when people come in at odd times for meals. This recipe will make eight such pizzas: divide the mixture into eight pieces instead of four and roll each into a circle about 10cm (4 in) across. Complete each with the topping, as described above, then open-freeze the pizzas. When they're frozen they can be packed in a polythene bag and used one by one as required. They can be cooked in a frying pan and finished off under the grill, and take about 15 minutes from frozen. When I'm feeling keen I make a double batch (twice the quantities given above) and stock up the freezer – but they don't last long!

Rice, Pasta, Egg and Cheese Dishes

This section contains a variety of recipes, ranging from the simple, quick-to-make cheese fondue to the more elaborate stuffed pancakes, mushroom rice and lasagne. With the exception of Scotch eggs, which are useful for picnics and buffet parties, all the recipes make good supper dishes and though they may be a little effort to make they can be served simply with a green salad.

The lentil and wine sauce for spaghetti and the lasagne both freeze very well but it's best to put the quick topping on the lasagne just before you bake it.

CHEESE FONDUE

This is such a useful dish for those occasions when you have to make something delicious and a bit special on the spur of the moment. As fondues are rich, I like to start with a light, fruity first course such as pineapple wedges or melon with strawberries and then have a refreshing salad after the fondue. If you want to serve a pudding course, a tart such as the blackcurrant lattice or Bakewell tart go well, or, for something lighter, a fruit sorbet.

Serves 4–6

1 garlic clove
275ml ($^1/_2$ pint) dry white wine
    or cider
225g (8 oz) Gruyère cheese and
    225g (8 oz) Emmenthal
    cheese, grated; *or* use 450g
    (1 lb) vegetarian Cheddar
    cheese, grated
1 tablespoon cornflour
1–2 tablespoons kirsch –
    optional

sea salt and freshly ground black
    pepper
grated nutmeg
1 large French loaf *or* crusty
    wholewheat loaf – *or* half of
    each – cut into bite-sized
    pieces and warmed in the
    oven

Halve the garlic and rub the cut surfaces over the inside of a medium-sized saucepan (or special fondue pan). Put the wine or cider and cheese into the saucepan and heat gently, stirring all the time until the cheese has melted. Mix the cornflour to a paste with the kirsch if you're using it, or use a drop more wine or cider; pour this paste into the cheese mixture, stirring all the time until you have a lovely creamy consistency. Occasionally, the cheese goes all lumpy and stringy at this point. Don't despair; if you beat it vigorously for a moment or two with a rotary whisk all will be well. Season the fondue then place the saucepan over the lighted burner and let everyone start dipping their bread into the delicious mixture.

MUSHROOM RICE WITH ALMOND AND RED PEPPER

The secret of this recipe is to use plenty of mushrooms and to cook them thoroughly, separately from the rice, so that you get a really rich flavour and a tender moist texture. This is a nice easy-going dish because if necessary you can cover it with foil and keep it warm for a while in a cool oven. It only really needs some grated Parmesan and a well-dressed green salad to go with it, though I must admit that for a special occasion I also like it with some rich-tasting Béarnaise sauce! There is some protein in the almonds, rice and Parmesan, but for a well-balanced meal it would be a good idea to introduce some more either in the first course or the pudding, or add some little cubes of cheese or cooked haricot beans to the salad.

Serves 4–6

225g (8 oz) long grain brown rice
575ml (1 pint) dry cider *or* good
vegetable stock, *or* a mixture
sea salt
25g (1 oz) butter
3 tablespoons oil
1 large onion, peeled and
chopped
900g (2 lb) button mushrooms,
washed and sliced

2 large garlic cloves, peeled and
crushed
50g (2 oz) blanched almonds, cut
lengthwise into slivers
1 medium-sized red pepper,
de-seeded and chopped
freshly ground black pepper
fresh parsley, chopped
Parmesan cheese, grated

Put the rice into a medium-sized, heavy-based saucepan and add the cider, stock or stock and cider and a level teaspoon of sea salt. Bring to the boil, give the rice a quick stir, then cover the saucepan, turn the heat right down and leave the rice to cook very gently for 45 minutes. Then take the saucepan off the heat and leave to stand, still covered, for a further 15 minutes.

While this is happening, heat the butter and 1 tablespoonful of the oil in a large saucepan and fry the onion for 5 minutes, until beginning to soften; then put in the mushrooms and garlic and cook for a further 20–25 minutes, stirring from time to time, until all the liquid has disappeared and the mushrooms are dark and glossy-looking.

Heat the rest of the oil in another small saucepan or frying pan and first fry the almonds until golden, then take them out and place on to a piece of kitchen paper. Quickly fry the red pepper, for about 5 minutes, just to soften it a little.

To complete the dish, add the mushrooms, red peppers and almonds to the cooked rice, using if possible a wooden fork to avoid mashing the rice. Season carefully with salt and plenty of freshly ground black pepper. Spoon the mixture on to a large, warmed plate or shallow ovenproof dish and sprinkle with freshly chopped parsley. Serve with Parmesan cheese.

VEGETARIAN SCOTCH EGGS

Scotch eggs look attractive when they're sliced, and are useful for picnics and buffets. The secret of getting the outside to stick to the egg is to dip the hardboiled egg into beaten egg before putting the coating on. The protein content of these Scotch eggs is excellent and they're good for lunch boxes, with some nice crisp salad.

Makes 4

1 onion, peeled and grated
50g (2 oz) roasted hazel nuts, grated
50g (2 oz) ground almonds
50g (2 oz) cheese, grated
2 heaped teaspoons tomato purée
1 egg
1 tablespoon fresh thyme, chopped *or* 1 teaspoon dried
sea salt and freshly ground black pepper
4 hardboiled eggs, shelled
beaten egg and crisp wholewheat crumbs to coat
fat for deep-frying

First make the outside coating for the Scotch eggs; simply mix the onion, nuts, cheese, tomato purée, egg and thyme together to a fairly firm paste and season, adding a tablespoonful of stock, water or cider to soften the consistency a little if necessary.

To finish the eggs, dip the whole hardboiled eggs in beaten egg and then press the nut mixture round to cover them completely. Coat the Scotch eggs in egg and breadcrumbs. Heat the oil in a deep frying pan to a temperature of 190°C (375°F), then deep-fry the Scotch eggs for 2–3 minutes, until golden brown and crisp, and drain on crumpled kitchen paper. Leave the Scotch eggs until they are cool, then cut each in half or into quarters and serve with salad.

LENTIL LASAGNE

This dish consists of layers of lasagne and a tasty mixture of lentils, tomatoes and wine, topped with cheese sauce. I must admit that, contrary to my wholefood principles, I prefer this dish made with white lasagne rather than the wholewheat type, although it works with either. If you use white lasagne you can replace some fibre by adding a final topping of wholewheat breadcrumbs mixed with a tablespoon of fine bran if you want to. The lasagne can be made in advance and only needs a crisp green salad and perhaps some red wine or cider to go with it.

Serves 4–6

2 tablespoons oil
1 onion, peeled and chopped
2 garlic cloves, peeled and crushed
1 medium-large red *or* green pepper, de-seeded and chopped
175g (6 oz) split red lentils
425g (15 oz) can tomatoes
1 bay leaf
275ml (1/2 pint) vegetable stock *or* water
2 tablespoons tomato purée

150ml (1/4 pint) red wine *or* dry cider
1/4 teaspoon each of dried oregano, thyme and basil
1/2 teaspoon cinnamon
15g (1/2 oz) butter
1 tablespoon fresh parsley, chopped
sea salt and freshly ground black pepper
sugar
175g (6 oz) lasagne

For the topping

2 eggs
150ml (1/4 pint) milk

225g (8 oz) *fromage blanc*
125g (4 oz) cheese, grated

Heat the oil in a medium-sized saucepan and fry the onion for 10 minutes, then add the garlic, pepper, lentils, tomatoes, bay leaf, stock or water and tomato purée. Bring to the boil and simmer gently for 20–30 minutes, until the lentils are tender and most of the water absorbed. Remove the bay leaf, and stir in the wine or cider, herbs, cinnamon, butter and chopped parsley. Mix well, then add salt, pepper and a little sugar to taste.

While the lentil mixture is cooking, prepare the lasagne. Half fill a large saucepan with lightly salted water and bring to the boil. Ease the pieces of lasagne into the boiling water and cook them for about 8 minutes, until they are just tender, then drain and drape the pieces of lasagne round the edge of the colander so they don't stick together.

Set the oven to 200°C (400°F), gas mark 6. Put a layer of lasagne in the base of a shallow ovenproof dish and cover with half the lentil mixture; follow this with another layer of lasagne, followed by the rest of the lentils, finishing with a layer of lasagne. Whisk together the eggs, milk and *fromage blanc*, season lightly and pour this over the top. Sprinkle with the grated cheese. Bake for about 45 minutes, until golden brown and bubbling.

Lentil lasagne freezes very well, without the topping.

BAKED PANCAKES WITH LEEKS

This is a useful dish because it can be prepared in advance and then just heated through in a moderate oven when you want it. It only needs a green salad to go with it.

Serves 6–8

For the pancakes

50g (2 oz) plain wholewheat flour
a pinch of sea salt
2 eggs

1 tablespoon oil
150ml (^{1}/4 pint) milk
extra oil for frying

For the filling

900g (2 lb) leeks
15g (^{1}/2 oz) butter
1 tablespoon fresh parsley, chopped

sea salt and freshly ground black pepper

For the topping

2 eggs
150ml (¹/₄ pint) milk

225g (8 oz) *fromage blanc*
125g (4 oz) cheese, grated

First make the pancake batter: the easiest way to do this is to put all the ingredients into the liquidizer and blend to a smooth, creamy mixture. If you haven't a liquidizer, put the flour and salt into a bowl, break in the eggs and beat, then gradually mix in the oil and milk to make a smooth, creamy consistency.

To make the pancakes, brush a small frying pan with a little oil and set it over a moderate heat. When it's hot, pour in 2 tablespoons of the batter, then tip and swirl the pan so that the mixture runs all over the base. Then put the pan over the heat for 20–30 seconds until the top of the pancake is set and the underside is flecked golden brown. Flip the pancake over using a small palette knife and your fingers if necessary. Cook the other side of the pancake, then lift it out on to a plate. Brush the frying pan with more oil if necessary and make another pancake in the same way, putting it on top of the first pancake when it's done. Continue until you have finished all the mixture and have about twelve thin pancakes.

Next make the filling. Wash and slice the leeks, then cook them in a little fast-boiling salted water for about 10 minutes, until just tender. Drain well and add the butter, parsley and salt and pepper to taste.

Set the oven to 180°C (350°F), gas mark 4. Put a heaped tablespoon of the leek mixture on each pancake, roll the pancake neatly and place it in a large, greased, shallow casserole dish. Make the topping by quickly beating together the eggs, milk and *fromage blanc*, season lightly and pour this over the pancakes. Sprinkle with the grated cheese, cover the dish with a piece of foil and bake the pancakes for 40–45 minutes, removing the foil about 15 minutes before the end of the cooking time to brown the cheese on top.

A pleasant variation is to use home-made tomato sauce instead of the creamy sauce.

SPAGHETTI WITH LENTIL AND WINE SAUCE

This is a delicious spaghetti dish with a rich-tasting lentil and tomato sauce. The protein in the spaghetti complements that of the lentils, with a bit more from the cheese besides, so this dish represents excellent nourishment. The lentil sauce can be made in advance, if convenient, and reheated when you need it. Serve with a green salad with a good garlicky dressing and some robust red wine and finish with fruit or some good cheese – or ice cream if you're in the mood and want to keep the Italian theme – for a lovely cheap and comforting meal.

Serves 3–4

1 tablespoon olive oil
1 onion, peeled and chopped
1 large garlic clove, peeled and crushed
1 teaspoon basil
225g (8 oz) tomatoes, peeled and chopped – *or* use a small can, drained
125g (4 oz) continental 'brown' or 'green' lentils

1 tablespoon tomato purée
275ml (^{1}/2 pint) cheap red wine *or* dry cider
275ml (^{1}/2 pint) vegetable stock
sea salt and freshly ground black pepper
225g (8 oz) spaghetti
butter
Parmesan cheese, grated

Heat the oil in a medium-sized saucepan and fry the onion for 10 minutes, until softened and lightly browned. Add the garlic, basil, tomatoes, lentils, tomato purée, wine or cider and stock. Bring to the boil, then put a lid on the saucepan, turn down the heat and leave to cook gently for about 45 minutes, stirring from time to time, until the lentils are tender and the mixture is reduced to a thick purée. Season with sea salt and plenty of freshly ground black pepper. Just before the lentil mixture is done, cook the spaghetti in plenty of boiling salted water, page 155; drain well, return the spaghetti to the hot saucepan with a knob of butter and turn the spaghetti so that it all gets coated with the melted butter and looks glossy and appetizing. Put the spaghetti on a large, heated dish, pour the lentil sauce on top and sprinkle with grated Parmesan cheese.

Sauces and Salad Dressings

This section contains the sauces which are useful for serving with the salads, savouries and puddings in this book.

With the exception of mayonnaise and Béarnaise sauce, the sauces are mostly simple and light, based on fruit and vegetable purées or mixtures of soured cream, natural yoghurt and *fromage blanc*. I also find yoghurt and *fromage blanc* most useful for adding to classic mayonnaise or Béarnaise sauce to lighten them when less richness is required.

APPLE AND CRANBERRY SAUCE

If you use sweet apples for this recipe, they take off some of the sharpness of the cranberries so you need less sugar, and the result is a pleasant, fruity sauce that's ideal with nut roasts.

Serves 6

450g (1 lb) sweet apples	ground cinnamon
125g (4 oz) cranberries	ground cloves
25–50g (1–2 oz) sugar	

Peel, core and slice the apples. Wash and pick over the cranberries, removing any stems. Put the apples and cranberries into a small, heavy-based saucepan with the sugar and cook over a gentle heat, with a lid on the saucepan, for about 10 minutes until soft and mushy. Mash the fruits with a spoon or liquidize if you prefer a smooth sauce. Taste the mixture and add a little more sugar if necessary, and a pinch of ground cinnamon or cloves if you like the flavour.

APPLE AND REDCURRANT SAUCE

This is made in the same way, using redcurrants instead of the cranberries. You can also make a pleasant sauce by just softening the apples in two rounded tablespoons of redcurrant (or cranberry) jelly and leaving out the sugar.

BREAD SAUCE

1 onion, peeled
3 cloves
275ml (^{1}/2 pint) milk
1 bay leaf
50g (2 oz) fresh white bread,
 crusts removed

15g (^{1}/2 oz) butter
1–2 tablespoons cream
sea salt, freshly ground black
 pepper
grated nutmeg

Put the onion, studded with the cloves, into a saucepan and add the milk and bay leaf. Bring to the boil, then take off the heat, add the slices of bread, cover and leave on one side for 15–30 minutes for the flavours to infuse. Then remove the onion and bay leaf, beat the mixture to break up the bread and stir in the butter, cream and salt, pepper and nutmeg to taste. If you are making the sauce in advance, once you have beaten it smooth you can put back the onion and bay leaf, so that they can continue to flavour the sauce until you're ready to serve it.

SPECIAL WINE SAUCE

Makes 300ml (^{1}/2 pint)

15g (^{1}/2 oz) butter
1 tablespoon oil
1 small onion, peeled and
 chopped
1 large garlic clove, peeled and
 crushed
2 large tomatoes, chopped,
 preferably fresh (unpeeled) *or*
 canned ones, drained

400ml (^{3}/4 pint) vegetable stock
150ml (^{1}/4 pint) red wine *or* cider
sea salt and freshly ground black
 pepper

Heat the butter and oil in a medium-sized saucepan and fry the onion for 5 minutes without browning. Add the garlic and tomatoes, and cook for a further 3–4 minutes. Then pour in the stock and wine or cider and let the mixture bubble away until the liquid has reduced by about half. Strain and season with salt and freshly ground black pepper.

MUSHROOM AND SOURED CREAM SAUCE

This is a creamy fresh-tasting sauce that's best served warm and is delicious with nutmeats, burgers and also with plainly cooked vegetables.

Serves 4–6

15g (¹/₂ oz) butter
125g (4 oz) button mushrooms,
  washed and chopped
150ml (¹/₄ pint) soured cream

sea salt and freshly ground black
  pepper
paprika

Melt the butter in a medium-sized saucepan and fry the mushrooms for about 5 minutes, then stir in the soured cream and salt, pepper and a little paprika to taste. Reheat gently, but don't let the sauce get too near boiling point.

SOURED CREAM AND HERB SAUCE

This sauce is served cold, but I like it with hot dishes, such as the savoury loaves, as well as with cold ones.

Makes 275 ml (¹/₂ pint)

150ml (¹/₄ pint) soured cream
150ml (¹/₄ pint) natural yoghurt
2 tablespoons fresh herbs,
  chopped: parsley, chives,
  tarragon, a little thyme –
  whatever is available

sea salt and freshly ground black
  pepper

Simply mix everything together and season to taste.

YOGHURT AND FRESH HERB SAUCE

This is made in exactly the same way except that you use 275ml ($^1/_2$ pint) natural yoghurt and leave out the soured cream; a tablespoonful of single cream can be stirred in for added richness. I like it particularly with chopped mint or green fennel, for serving with lentil rissoles or new potatoes.

YOGHURT AND CUCUMBER SAUCE

For this variation, which is delicate and refreshing, use 275ml ($^1/_2$ pint) natural yoghurt, 3–4 tablespoons finely chopped cucumber and 1 tablespoon chopped fresh fennel, dill, mint or whatever other fresh herb you fancy.

YOGHURT AND SPRING ONION SAUCE

Make as above, using 275ml ($^1/_2$ pint) natural yoghurt and 3 tablespoons chopped spring onions.

TOMATO SAUCE

I find this one of the most useful sauces as it seems to go with so many different dishes. It's best made from fresh tomatoes, and even imported winter tomatoes give a good result – better than canned ones.

Makes about 400 ml (³/4 pint)

1 tablespoon oil
1 onion, peeled and chopped
1 garlic clove, peeled and
  crushed
450g (1 lb) tomatoes, peeled and
  chopped, *or* 425g (15 oz) can

sea salt and freshly ground black
  pepper
2–3 tablespoons red wine *or*
  cider – optional

Heat the oil in a medium-sized saucepan and fry the onion for 10 minutes, until softened but not browned. Add the garlic and tomatoes, and cook for a further 15 minutes, until the tomatoes have collapsed and reduced to a purée. Sieve or liquidize the mixture and season with salt and pepper. This is nice sometimes with a dash of wine or cider added.

BLENDER BÉARNAISE SAUCE

This is a quick version of this classic, rich, creamy sauce: you first reduce the vinegar in a saucepan to concentrate the flavour, then add it to the egg yolks in the liquidizer and pour in the melted butter. It only takes a few minutes to make and is superb for a special occasion: I love it with the white nutmeat with capers on page 130. A very pleasant variation is to stir 125g (4 oz) *fromage blanc* into the finished sauce – this lightens it, and with this addition the quantities given below will serve eight people.

Serves 6

125g (4 oz) butter
2 tablespoons wine vinegar
1 tablespoon very finely
  chopped onion
8 peppercorns, lightly crushed

2 egg yolks
1 tablespoon lemon juice
sea salt and freshly ground black
  pepper

Melt the butter in a small saucepan. Heat the vinegar, onion and peppercorns together in a small saucepan until the vinegar has reduced by half. Put the egg yolks and lemon juice into the liquidizer goblet and blend until just creamy, then strain in the vinegar mixture and blend again. Now, with the liquidizer still going, pour the melted butter slowly in through the top of the goblet. As you do so the mixture will thicken to a beautiful creamy consistency. Season with salt and pepper and serve immediately, just warm. If you need to keep this sauce warm, the safest way is to stand the saucepan in another larger saucepan or roasting tin containing very hot water.

MAYONNAISE – BLENDER METHOD

Here again, the use of a liquidizer makes it easy to produce creamy, successful results every time.

Makes 200ml (7 fl oz)

1 whole egg
1/4 teaspoon salt
1/4 teaspoon dry mustard
2 or 3 grindings of black pepper
2 teaspoons wine vinegar

2 teaspoons lemon juice
200ml (7 fl oz) olive oil *or* a
   mixture of olive oil and soya
   or sunflower oil

Break the egg straight into the liquidizer and add the salt, mustard, pepper, vinegar and lemon juice. Blend for a minute at medium speed until everything is well mixed, then turn the speed up to high and gradually add the oil, drop by drop, through the hole in the lid of the liquidizer goblet. When you've added about half the oil you will hear the sound change to a 'glug-glug' noise and then you can add the rest of the oil more quickly, in a thin stream. If the consistency of the mayonnaise seems a bit on the thick side, you can thin it with a little boiling water or some milk.

MAYONNAISE – TRADITIONAL METHOD

It's more work to make mayonnaise by hand, but you do get a beautiful, creamy result and it's very satisfying to see the mixture gradually thicken as you whisk in the oil.

Makes 200–275ml (7–10 fl oz)

2–3 egg yolks
$^1/_4$ teaspoon salt
$^1/_4$ teaspoon dry mustard
2 or 3 grindings of black pepper
2 teaspoons wine vinegar

2 teaspoons lemon juice
200–275ml (7 fl oz) olive oil *or* a
    mixture of olive oil and soya
    or sunflower oil

Put the egg yolks into a bowl and add the salt, mustard, pepper, vinegar and lemon juice. Whisk for a minute or two until everything is well mixed and creamy, then start to add the oil, just a drop at a time, whisking hard after each addition. When you have added about half the oil the mixture will begin to thicken and look like mayonnaise, and then you can add the oil a little more quickly, still whisking hard. Go on adding the oil until the mixture is really thick – if you use three egg yolks you will probably be able to use the full amount of oil, otherwise about 200ml (7 fl oz) will be enough. If the consistency of the mayonnaise seems a bit on the thick side, you can thin it with a little boiling water or some milk.

LEMON MAYONNAISE SAUCE

This sauce tastes creamy yet is light and refreshing. You can serve it cold, with dishes like the walnut pâté en croûte, or use it to coat lightly cooked vegetables before topping with crumbs and grated cheese and baking, for an extra special *au gratin* dish.

Serves 4–6

4 tablespoons mayonnaise
6 tablespoons *fromage blanc*
1 teaspoon mustard

juice of $1/2$ lemon
sea salt and freshly ground black
  pepper

Just mix everything together to a smooth cream and season to taste.

VINAIGRETTE

When I'm making this to dress a salad, I usually make it straight into the salad bowl, mix quickly and put the salad in on top. But if you need it for pouring over a salad, or for serving with avocados, for instance, it's easiest to make it by shaking all the ingredients together in a clean screw-top jar, and for this you may want to double the quantities given here. (Any that's over will keep in the fridge, but I think it's very much better made fresh when you need it and it only takes a moment.)

1 tablespoon wine vinegar –
  preferably red
3–4 tablespoons best quality
  olive oil

sea salt and freshly ground black
  pepper

Mix everything together, adding plenty of seasoning. Some chopped fresh herbs, also a little mustard and a dash of sugar can be added to vary the flavour.

BRANDY BUTTER

If you want to make a polyunsaturated version of this, use unsalted polyunsaturated margarine from the health shop; and for a less rich result you can replace half the butter (or margarine) with curd cheese or *fromage blanc*.

Sauces and Salad Dressings

Serves 6

125g (4 oz) unsalted butter *or*
  polyunsaturated margarine
25–50g (1–2 oz) icing sugar *or*
  soft brown sugar

1–2 tablespoons brandy

Beat the butter or margarine until creamy, then beat in 25g (1 oz) of the icing or soft brown sugar: taste, and add a little more if you want a sweeter result. Add the brandy and beat again to make a light, fluffy cream. Put the mixture into a small serving dish and chill until required.

Puddings

This is the time when, with everyone feeling relaxed, happy and well fed, you have the opportunity to have fun and end the meal in a memorable way. That doesn't mean to say that the pudding needs to be complicated or difficult to make; some of the most spectacular ones are also some of the simplest. Fragrant rose sorbet, for instance, or peaches in strawberry purée.

But it is also rewarding to try and think of an unusual way of flavouring or garnishing an ordinary pudding to make it a bit different or amusing: putting cheesecake on a chocolate base and rippling the top with sharp-tasting fruit purée, or sticking strawberries into a cone of creamy curd cheese to make a mountain, for instance; adding spice to a homely baked crumble topping or serving ice cream with a hot chestnut and brandy sauce.

Ices and Sorbets

BLACKCURRANT SORBET WITH CASSIS

I use bought bottled blackcurrants for this, but fresh ones, home-bottled or frozen ones would be even better. You could leave out the cassis, but it is lovely if you are serving this for a special occasion. It can also be added to chilled dry white wine to make the pretty pink aperitif Kir: see page 28.

Serves 6

450g (1 lb) fresh blackcurrants
and 125g (4 oz) sugar; *or* 2 x
375g (13 oz) bottles
blackcurrants in syrup

2 egg whites
6 tablespoons cassis
a little lightly-whipped cream –
optional

First find a shallow plastic container which will hold 1 litre (2 pints) and put this into the coldest part of the fridge to chill. Next prepare the blackcurrants. If you're using fresh ones, rinse them under cold water and take off the little stalks. Put them into a heavy-based saucepan with 125g (4 oz) sugar and cook them over a gentle heat for 10–15 minutes until soft. Liquidize the blackcurrants, together with their juice, then push them through a sieve to make a smooth, thick purée. Take out 3 tablespoons of this and keep on one side for the sauce, then pour the rest into the chilled container and freeze until there is a solid layer about 2.5cm (1 in) round the edges; break it up with a fork. Whisk the egg whites until stiff and standing in peaks but not dry, then add the frozen blackcurrant purée, still whisking, to make a thick, fluffy mixture. Pour this back into the container and freeze again until solid. Next make a simple sauce by mixing the reserved purée with the cassis.

Take the sorbet out of the coldest part of the fridge and stand it on a shelf in the fridge an hour before you want to eat it, to give it time to soften a little. Put spoonfuls of the sorbet in individual glasses and pour 1½ tablespoons of the sauce over each; top with a little cream if liked.

MELON SORBET WITH
CRYSTALLIZED MINT LEAVES

This is prettiest if you can find two small melons with flesh of contrasting colours, orange and pale green. Make the sorbet in two separate containers and put a spoonful of both in each bowl. Leave out the mint leaves if you haven't time to do them; but they are pretty for a special occasion and can be made in advance and stored in an airtight tin.

Serves 6

2 small ripe melons, if possible
    one with orange flesh and one
    with green, each weighing
    about 700g (1½ lb)

2 tablespoons fresh lemon juice
50g (2 oz) sugar
2 egg whites

For the mint leaves

20 fresh mint leaves
1 egg white

granulated sugar

Halve the melons, take out the seeds and then scoop all the flesh from the skins, keeping the two colours separate. Liquidize the chunks of scooped-out melon, add half the lemon juice and half the sugar to each; taste and add a little more sugar if necessary.

170

Turn the two mixtures into separate containers, then freeze and finish as for blackcurrant sorbet, adding half the egg white to each bowl.

About an hour before you want to eat the sorbet, take the containers of sorbet out of the coldest part of the fridge and stand them on a shelf in the fridge to give them time to soften a little. Put alternate spoonfuls of each colour in individual glasses and garnish with the mint leaves.

To make the mint leaves, first wash the leaves and pat dry with kitchen paper. Beat the egg white lightly, just to break it up. Have a saucer of sugar ready. Brush the mint leaves all over with egg white then dip them into the sugar, coating them on both sides. Lay the leaves on a piece of greaseproof or silicon paper on a dry baking sheet and put them into a very cool oven, 120°C (250°F), gas mark ¹/₂, for about 2 hours to dry out, until they are crisp and brittle. Cool, then store in an airtight tin until needed.

ROSE SORBET

I wanted to make a pudding that would look like pink roses, for a summer meal, and this is the result: a delicate pink sorbet that is served in small bowls, with rose leaves round the outside, to resemble the calyx of the rose. Although my original idea was to make this sorbet with fragrant red rose petals from the summer garden, I have found that you can make it equally well in winter without using any rose petals because most of the flavour and fragrance comes from the rose water, but you will need to use some other non-poisonous leaves to decorate the bowls (or leave this out).

Serves 4–6

a handful of perfumed, red rose petals

550ml (1 pint) water

125g (4 oz) granulated sugar

3–4 tablespoons rose water

a little pink vegetable colouring – optional

2 egg whites

a few bright green, glossy rose leaves

First find a shallow plastic container which will hold 1 litre (2 pints) and put this into the coldest part of the fridge to chill. Next wash the rose petals gently, then put them into a saucepan with the water. Bring up to the boil, then cover and leave for 15–30 minutes for the rose petals to infuse the water. Strain through a sieve, pressing as much of the water out of the petals as you can. Measure the water and if necessary make up to 550ml (1 pint) with a little cold water. Put this into a saucepan with the sugar and heat gently until the sugar has dissolved. Add the rose water and a few drops of colouring to intensify the pink of the syrup if necessary – remember it will be further toned-down when the egg whites are added. Remove from the heat and leave to cool, then pour into the chilled container and freeze until there is a solid layer about 2.5cm (1 in) round the edges; break it up with a fork. Whisk the egg whites until stiff and standing in peaks, but not dry, then add the frozen rose syrup, still whisking, to make a thick fluffy mixture. Pour this back into the container and freeze again until solid. Take the sorbet out of the coldest part of the fridge and stand it on a shelf in the fridge an hour before you want to eat it, to give it time to soften a little. Put spoonfuls of the sorbet in individual glasses and tuck a few fresh green rose leaves around the edge of each, to give a rosebud effect.

STRAWBERRY SORBET WITH KIWI FRUIT

I think this sorbet is one way of getting the best from frozen strawberries, because for this their mushiness is actually an advantage! The sorbet looks so pretty served in a border of sliced green kiwi fruit.

Serves 6

450g (1 lb) fresh *or* frozen strawberries, thawed
1 tablespoon fresh lemon juice

125g (4 oz) sugar
2 egg whites
3 kiwi fruit

Liquidize and sieve the strawberries, adding the lemon juice to bring out the flavour and enough sugar to sweeten, then make the sorbet exactly as for blackcurrant sorbet, page 169.

About an hour before you want to eat the sorbet, take it out of the coldest part of the fridge and stand it on a shelf in the fridge to give it time to soften a little. Peel the kiwi fruits and cut them into thin slices. Put spoonfuls of the sorbet in individual glasses and tuck the kiwi fruit round the edge.

CHESTNUT ICE CREAM

This is a beautiful ice cream with a delicate flavour. These quantities make a generous amount of ice cream and you could halve them if you prefer; half this would be enough for four people but I don't think it's quite enough for six. If you want to make a less-rich, healthier version, half whipping cream and half *fromage blanc* works very well.

Serves 8

425g (15 oz) can chestnut purée
575ml (1 pint) whipping cream

175g (6 oz) caster sugar
4 tablespoons brandy

Put the chestnut purée into a bowl or the bowl of your mixer and beat until smooth. Then add the cream, sugar and brandy and beat everything together until thick, smooth and standing in peaks. Turn mixture into a plastic container and freeze until solid. There is no need to stir the mixture during freezing, but do take it out of the fridge at the beginning of the meal and beat it before serving as it is much nicer if it is not too solid.

RASPBERRY ICE CREAM

This is a favourite ice cream. It is quite rich, but, as with the chestnut ice cream, I have found that you can reduce the amount of cream and use half cream and half *fromage blanc* for a lighter, healthier version.

Serves 6

225g (8 oz) fresh *or* frozen
   raspberries, thawed
125g (4 oz) sugar

275ml (1/2 pint) whipping cream
   – *or* use half cream and half
   fromage blanc

Liquidize, then sieve the raspberries to remove the pips and make a smooth purée. Add the sugar. Whisk the cream until thick, then add the *fromage blanc*, if you're using it, and whisk again until soft peaks are formed. Fold this cream gently but thoroughly into the raspberry purée. Turn the mixture into a plastic container and put in the coldest part of the fridge. Leave until half frozen, then remove from the container and beat well. Return mixture to the freezing compartment and leave until completely frozen.

   This ice cream is best if it's not too hard; put it into the normal part of the fridge for about an hour before you need it to let it 'come to' before serving.

VANILLA ICE CREAM WITH
HOT CHESTNUT AND BRANDY SAUCE

In this recipe, smooth, creamy, vanilla ice cream is topped with a hot sauce made from chestnut purée with wine and brandy. It is a wonderful pudding for special occasions.

Serves 4–6

2 eggs *or* 4 egg yolks
275ml (¹/2 pint) milk
75g (3 oz) vanilla sugar *or* caster
  sugar plus a few drops of
  vanilla essence

275ml (¹/2 pint) whipping cream

For the sauce

125g (4 oz) canned, unsweetened
  chestnut purée
200ml (7 fl oz) white wine *or*
  cider

25g (1 oz) sugar
3 tablespoons brandy

Whisk the eggs in a medium-sized bowl. Put the milk and sugar into a heavy-based saucepan and bring just up to the boil, then slowly add it to the eggs, stirring all the time. Strain the eggs and milk back into the saucepan, put back on the heat and stir for just a minute or two until the mixture thickens: this happens very quickly, so watch it and stir all the time. Leave this custard to cool.

Whisk the cream until it has thickened and is standing in soft peaks, then fold this gently but thoroughly into the cooled egg custard. Pour the mixture into a plastic container and freeze until it's setting well round the edges. Then scrape the ice cream into a bowl and whisk it thoroughly. Put the ice cream back into the container and freeze until it's firm. Take the ice cream out of the fridge at the beginning of the meal and beat it before serving as it is much nicer if it is not too solid.

To make the sauce, put the chestnut purée into a saucepan and break it up with a fork; then gradually stir in the wine or cider and the sugar. Set the pan over a gentle heat and stir until you have a thick, creamy consistency: this can all be done well in advance. Just before you want to serve the ice cream, reheat the chestnut mixture, beating it smooth, and add the brandy.

Again, you can make this ice cream with half cream and half *fromage blanc* if preferred, and the results are very good.

Fruity Puddings

SPECIAL FRUIT SALAD

I think a fresh fruit salad, made with interesting fruits which contrast and complement each other in colour and flavour, is one of the most delicious puddings. The exact composition depends, of course, on what is available, but I like to include strawberries, black grapes or cherries when possible, and also kiwi fruit because its vivid green provides such a pretty colour contrast. The apricot liqueur gives a lovely flavour and draws out the juices from the fruits, and it's also good made with one of the orange liqueurs, such as cointreau, but if you don't want to use liqueur you could use sweet white wine or orange juice.

Serves 6–8

4 kiwi fruit	1 medium-sized ripe pineapple
225g (8 oz) strawberries	275ml (¹/₂ pint) apricot juice
2 medium-sized ripe mangoes	6–8 tablespoons apricot liqueur

Peel the kiwi fruits and cut the flesh into thin rounds; wash and hull the strawberries, halving or quartering any large ones; cut the mangoes in half and remove the stone; peel the flesh and cut into dice; peel and dice the pineapple, cutting away any hard central core. Put all the fruit into a serving dish and add the apricot juice and liqueur. Chill the fruit salad until required –

it's best if you can let it stand for a couple of hours so that the juices can be drawn out and the flavours can blend.

FRESH MANGOES

If you can find some really ripe medium-sized mangoes, they make a lovely pudding that's very simple to do and yet which always seems to please people. The mangoes should feel really soft to the touch; like avocados they will ripen in the airing cupboard if put into a paper bag and left for two or three days.

1 medium-large mango serves 2 people

Don't prepare the mangoes until just before the meal. Then slice each mango down from the top, cutting about 6mm ($^1/_4$ in) each side of the stalk. The object of this is to make the cuts each side of the large flat stone in the centre. Ease the two halves apart and place each on a dish. You eat the mango as you would an avocado, by scooping the flesh out with a small spoon, and it's delicious.

PEACHES IN STRAWBERRY PURÉE

This dish consists of juicy, ripe peach slices bathed in a pink strawberry purée. It's another pudding that's very simple to do and a perfect way of using frozen strawberries. It's also delicious made with ripe comice pears instead of peaches.

Serves 6

6 large, ripe peaches – white	2 tablespoons lemon juice
ones are best if they're	450g (1 lb) ripe strawberries
available	50g (2 oz) sugar

Cover the peaches with boiling water; leave for 2 minutes, then drain. Slip the skins off using a sharp knife. Halve the peaches and remove the stones, then slice the flesh. Put the slices into a pretty glass bowl or six individual ones and sprinkle with half the lemon juice to preserve the colour.

Wash and hull the strawberries, then put them into a liquidizer with the rest of the lemon juice and reduce to a purée. Press the mixture through a sieve, to make it really smooth, then add the sugar gradually – taste the mixture, as you may not need it all. Pour the strawberry purée over the peaches.

PEARS IN CIDER WITH GINGER

The best pears for this are ones which are firm but sweet; if you don't like ginger you can leave it out.

Serves 6

6 firm, sweet pears, preferably	50g (2 oz) crystallized ginger,
conference	roughly chopped
850ml (1¹/₂ pints) sweet cider	

Peel the pears leaving them whole and with their stalks still attached. Put them into a large, heavy-based saucepan and pour in the cider – it should cover them. Bring them up to the boil, then turn the heat down and leave them to simmer, without a lid on the saucepan, for about 30 minutes, until the pears feel tender when pierced with a sharp knife and there is just a little syrupy-looking cider left. Add the ginger and leave to get completely cold. Serve chilled, with a bowl of lightly-whipped cream or chilled *fromage blanc*.

STUFFED PINEAPPLE HALVES

For this, small pineapples, one between two people, are halved right through the centre, including the leafy green top, then the flesh is cut and scooped out, mixed with black grapes or ripe strawberries and piled back in again. The stuffed pineapples look very pretty arranged like the spokes of a wheel on a large round plate.

Serves 6

3 small pineapples with attractive leafy tops

225g (8 oz) small, ripe strawberries *or* black grapes

Wash and dry the pineapples, then slice each in half right through the green top. Using a sharp knife and a spoon, scoop out the flesh and cut into small pieces, discarding any hard core. Wash the strawberries or grapes. Halve and stone the grapes; hull the strawberries and cut them as necessary. Mix the pineapple pieces with the strawberries or grapes and pile the mixture back into the skins. Arrange the stuffed pineapples on a large, flat plate.

RASPBERRIES IN REDCURRANT JELLY

This is a refreshing pudding: raspberries set in a clear jelly which is made from redcurrant juice. You can buy this at large supermarkets, and you can get agar agar, which is a powdered jelling agent, at health shops. This makes a jelly set very quickly, and if you are using frozen raspberries which haven't thawed, the jelly will set almost immediately, making this a good emergency dish!

Serves 6–8

350g (12 oz) fresh *or* frozen
  raspberries
700ml (24¹/2 fl oz) carton
  redcurrant juice
2 tablespoons sugar

2 level teaspoons agar agar
whipped cream
pistachio nuts, shelled and
  coarsely chopped

Divide the raspberries between six or eight small dishes. Put the redcurrant juice and sugar into a large saucepan and bring to the boil, then sprinkle the agar agar over the top, a little at a time, whisking after each addition to help the powder to dissolve. (The mixture will tend to froth up which is why you need a fairly large saucepan.) When all the agar agar has been added, let the mixture boil for 1 minute, then remove from the heat and strain over the raspberries. Leave to cool, then chill. Top the jellies with whipped cream and a few green pistachio nuts, shelled and chopped, to show their pretty green colour.

KIWI FRUIT IN GRAPE JELLY

Kiwi fruit is so pretty and this dish makes the most of its flower-like appearance.

Serves 6–8

4 kiwi fruit
700ml (25 fl oz) still, white grape
  juice
2 tablespoons sugar

2 level teaspoons agar agar
whipped cream
pistachio nuts, shelled and
  coarsely chopped

Make the jelly exactly as for raspberries in redcurrant jelly, arranging the slices of kiwi fruit attractively in the bowls.

APRICOT JELLY WITH FRESH APRICOTS AND STRAWBERRIES

For this jelly you need apricot juice, called 'apricot nectar' and available in a carton from large supermarkets and delicatessens.

Serves 6–8

8 ripe apricots
700ml (24^1/2 fl oz) carton apricot
   nectar
2 tablespoons sugar

2 level teaspoons agar agar
whipped cream
6–8 ripe strawberries to garnish

Skin the apricots by plunging them into boiling water for 2 minutes, then drain and slip off the skins with a sharp knife. Halve the apricots, remove the stones, then slice the flesh. Make the jelly exactly as for raspberries in redcurrant jelly. Put the apricots into the individual bowls, pour the apricot juice over and leave to set. Garnish with a swirl of whipped cream and some ripe strawberries.

RASPBERRY MERINGUE GÂTEAU

This is a superbly rich and indulgent pudding which nobody ought to eat but which everyone loves for a special occasion. It's also delicious made with sweet ripe blackberries, either freshly picked or frozen.

Serves 6

3 egg whites
175g (6 oz) caster sugar
275ml (^{1}/2 pint) whipping cream
  – *or*, if you want to make it
healthier, half whipping cream
and half *fromage blanc*

350g (12 oz) fresh *or* frozen
  raspberries, thawed
icing sugar

First make the meringue. Whisk the egg whites until stiff and dry, then whisk in half the sugar to make a smooth, glossy mixture. Fold in the rest of the sugar using a metal spoon. Draw two circles, 20cm (8 in) in diameter, on greaseproof, foil or silicon paper and brush with oil. Spoon the meringue to cover the circles in an even layer. Bake in a very cool oven, 120°C (250°F), gas mark ½, for 2–3 hours, until crisp and dry but not brown. Leave the meringue circles to cool completely, then peel off the paper. Store in an airtight tin until required for filling.

To fill the meringue, put one of the layers on a flat serving dish. Whip the cream, or cream and *fromage blanc*, until standing in soft peaks. Spread half this mixture over the meringue and top with half the raspberries. Cover with the other meringue circle and the rest of the cream and raspberries, and sieve a little icing sugar over the top. Serve as soon as possible.

STRAWBERRY MOUNTAIN

When strawberries are in season this makes an impressive pudding, a cone of strawberries stuck in a base of light creamy curd cheese. You can make the curd cheese base in advance, but it's best not to add the strawberries more than an hour before you want to serve the pudding. You must use double cream because the mixture needs to be firm. Needless to say, it's a very rich dish and I think the quantities given are just right for six people.

Serves 6

350g (12 oz) curd cheese   icing sugar
150ml (¼ pint) double cream
2 tablespoons vanilla sugar
450g (1 lb) small ripe
  strawberries, washed and
  hulled

Put the curd cheese into a bowl and beat with a spoon until smooth. Add the double cream and sugar and whisk together until light and thick enough to hold its shape well. Pile the mixture up into a cone shape on a flat serving dish. Chill until required. Just before you want to serve the pudding, stud the cone all over with the strawberries so that it is completely covered, and sift a little icing sugar over the top.

Pastries and Cheesecakes

ALMOND AND CHOCOLATE FLAN

This is an indulgent pudding for chocolate-lovers like me: a rich chocolate cream in a crisp case of light almond shortbread.

Serves 6–8

For the flan case

50g (2 oz) wholewheat flour
50g (2 oz) ground almonds
40g (1 1/2 oz) caster sugar

75g (3 oz) butter *or*
   polyunsaturated margarine

For the filling

175g (6 oz) plain chocolate
200ml (7 fl oz) whipping cream

First make the flan case. Set the oven to 180°C (350°F), gas mark 4. Grease a 20cm (8 in) round flan tin with butter. Put the flour, almonds and sugar into a bowl and gradually work in the butter or margarine to make a dough. Roll out to fit the flan tin; press gently into the tin, trim the edges and prick the base. Bake the flan for 25–30 minutes, until golden-brown and crisp. Cool.

   To make the filling, break the chocolate into a bowl, set the bowl over a saucepan of gently steaming water and leave until the chocolate has melted. Cool slightly, but do not allow to harden. Put the cream into another bowl, pour in the chocolate and whisk them together until you have a light, fluffy mixture. Pour this into the cooled flan dish. Chill until the chocolate mixture has set.

BAKEWELL TART

This traditional tart, with its crisp pastry covered with jam and a light almond sponge makes a very satisfactory pudding either hot or cold.

Serves 6

For the pastry

175g (6 oz) plain wholewheat flour
75g (3 oz) polyunsaturated margarine *or* butter

1¹/₂ tablespoons cold water

For the filling

3 tablespoons raspberry jam
125g (4 oz) soft margarine
125g (4 oz) caster sugar
2 eggs

25g (1 oz) plain flour
50g (2 oz) ground almonds
a few flaked almonds

First make the pastry: sift the flour into a large bowl, and just tip in the bran which will be left in the sieve. Rub the fat into the flour using your fingertips or a fork until the mixture resembles fine breadcrumbs – if the fat is soft you might find it easiest to start this process with a fork – then add the cold water and press the mixture together to form a dough. If there's time, leave this dough to rest for 30 minutes (this makes it easier to roll out but isn't essential).

Set the oven to 220°C (425°F), gas mark 7, and if possible place a heavy baking sheet on the top shelf to heat up with the oven. Roll out the pastry and ease it into a 20cm (8 in) lightly greased flan tin; trim edges. Spread with the jam. Put the margarine, sugar, eggs, flour and ground almonds into a bowl and beat for 2 minutes, until light and creamy. Spoon this mixture over the jam and sprinkle with a few flaked almonds. Bake in the pre-heated oven for 5 minutes, then turn the oven down to 180°C (350°F), gas mark 4, and bake for a further 30–35 minutes, until golden and firm to the touch. Serve hot or cold, with single cream if liked.

BLACKCURRANT LATTICE TART
WITH LEMON PASTRY

You could use a good quality blackcurrant jam (I like the Bulgarian ones) or one of the lovely no-added-sugar jams from health shops instead of the fruit, if you prefer: the tart is sweeter if you use jam.

Serves 6

For the pastry

175g (6 oz) plain wholewheat flour
finely grated rind of 1 lemon

75g (3 oz) polyunsaturated margarine *or* butter
1¹/₂ tablespoons cold water

For the filling

2 x 350g (12 oz) jars bottled blackcurrants, *or* about 350g (12 oz) fresh ones, topped and tailed

50–100g (2–4 oz) sugar
1 tablespoon cornflour
milk and extra sugar to glaze

First make the pastry: sift the flour into a large bowl, and just tip in the bran which will be left in the sieve. Add the lemon rind, then rub the fat into the flour using your fingertips or a fork until

186

the mixture resembles fine breadcrumbs – if the fat is soft you might find it easiest to start this process with a fork – then add the cold water and press the mixture together to form a dough. If there's time, leave this dough to rest for 30 minutes (this makes it easier to roll out but isn't essential).

Set the oven to 220°C (425°F), gas mark 7, and if possible place a heavy baking sheet on the top shelf to heat up with the oven. Roll out the pastry and ease it into a 20cm (8 in) lightly greased flan tin; trim edges.

Put the blackcurrants into a bowl and sprinkle with the sugar and cornflour. You will probably need the full amount of sugar for fresh blackcurrants but less for ones which have been bottled in a light syrup. Gently turn the blackcurrants so that they all get coated with the sugar and cornflour.

Spread the blackcurrants evenly in the flan case. Gather up and re-roll the pastry trimmings, cut into thin strips and arrange in a lattice on top of the blackcurrants. Brush the strips with milk and sprinkle with a little sugar. Bake in the pre-heated oven for 5 minutes, then turn the oven down to 180°C (350°F), gas mark 4, and bake for a further 30–5 minutes, until the pastry is golden brown. Serve hot or cold, with single cream if liked.

CHEESECAKE ON A CHOCOLATE BASE

This is a delicious cheesecake: a smooth cream cheese mixture swirled with sharp-tasting blackcurrant purée on a crisp base of chocolate and nuts. It's easy to make and needs no cooking.

Serves 6

For the base

125g (4 oz) digestive biscuits, crushed

50g (2 oz) chopped mixed nuts

125g (4 oz) plain chocolate, melted

For the filling

225g (8 oz) curd cheese   a little grated chocolate
275ml (^{1}/2 pint) whipping cream
25g (1 oz) sugar
3 tablespoons thick blackcurrant
  purée made by liquidizing then
  sieving the drained contents of
  a 375g (13 oz) jar of
  blackcurrants

First make the base: put all the ingredients into a bowl and mix together, then spread evenly in a 20cm (8 in) springclip tin or cake tin with a loose base. Leave in a cool place while you make the filling.

To make the filling, whip the curd cheese, cream and sugar together. Lightly mix in the blackcurrant purée, just swirling it. Don't mix it in too much. Pour the topping over the biscuit base. Chill for at least 2 hours, preferably overnight. Remove the sides of the tin; sprinkle with grated chocolate to serve.

STRAWBERRY CHEESECAKE

This recipe makes a big, luscious cheesecake with a shiny strawberry topping. It makes a wonderful pudding for a summer party.

Serves 8–10

175g (6 oz) digestive biscuits
75g (3 oz) soft butter *or* polyunsaturated margarine

For the filling

350g (12 oz) curd cheese   125g (4 oz) caster sugar
3 eggs   150ml (^{1}/4 pint) soured cream
1 teaspoon vanilla essence

For the topping

150ml (¹/₄ pint) soured cream   6–8 tablespoons redcurrant jelly
450g (1 lb) small ripe
   strawberries, washed and
   hulled

Set the oven to 150°C (300°F), gas mark 2. Put the digestive biscuits on a board and crush them with a rolling pin, then mix them with the butter or margarine. Press the biscuit mixture evenly into the base of a 20cm (8 in) springclip tin or cake tin with a removable base. Leave in a cool place while you make the filling.

To do this, if you've got a liquidizer, just put everything into the goblet and blend for a minute until smooth. Alternatively, put the curd cheese into a large bowl, then add the eggs, vanilla, caster sugar and soured cream and beat thoroughly to a smooth consistency. Pour the mixture into the tin on top of the crumbs.

Bake the cheesecake towards the bottom of the oven for 1¹/₂ hours, until it looks set and feels firm to a very light touch. Cool, then lightly beat the second carton of soured cream and spread over the top of the cheesecake. Chill for 2–3 hours.

To finish the cheesecake, arrange the strawberries evenly over the top. Melt the redcurrant jelly in a small, heavy-based saucepan over a gentle heat, then pour over the strawberries in a thin layer to glaze. Leave to cool, then carefully remove the cheesecake from the tin to serve.

JEWELLED FRUIT FLAN

Serves 6–8

For the flan case

75g (3 oz) wholewheat flour   125g (4 oz) butter *or*
75g (3 oz) ground almonds   polyunsaturated margarine
40g (1¹/₂ oz) caster sugar

For the filling

125g (4 oz) small, ripe strawberries, washed and hulled	125g (4 oz) redcurrants, topped and tailed
	6 tablespoons redcurrant jelly

First make the flan case. Set the oven to 180°C (350°F), gas mark 4. Grease a 20cm (8 in) round flan tin with butter. Put the flour, almonds and sugar into a bowl and gradually work in the butter or margarine to make a dough. Roll out fairly thickly to fit the flan tin; press gently into the tin, trim the edges and prick the base. Bake the flan for 25–30 minutes, until golden-brown and crisp. Cool.

To finish the flan, arrange the strawberries and redcurrants in alternate circles on top of the pastry, ending with a strawberry in the centre. Melt the redcurrant jelly in a small, heavy-based saucepan over a gentle heat, then pour evenly over the top of the fruit to glaze. Leave until the glaze has set.

Hot Puddings

GOURMET CHRISTMAS PUDDING

This recipe is an adaptation of Escoffier's Christmas pudding which I like because it is light both in flavour and texture.

Serves 8

225g (8 oz) fine wholewheat breadcrumbs – they must be soft and light

125g (4 oz) polyunsaturated margarine

125g (4 oz) wholewheat flour sifted with 1/2 teaspoon baking powder

2 teaspoons mixed spice

50g (2 oz) Barbados sugar

125g (4 oz) cooking apple, peeled and chopped

125g (4 oz) sultanas

125g (4 oz) raisins, seeded

125g (4 oz) currants

50g (2 oz) candied peel, chopped

50g (2 oz) crystallized ginger, chopped

grated rind of 1/2 small orange

grated rind of 1/2 small lemon

25g (1 oz) flaked almonds

1 egg

1 tablespoon orange juice

1 tablespoon lemon juice

4 tablespoons brandy

275ml (1/2 pint) brown ale

Put the breadcrumbs, margarine, flour, spice, sugar, apple, dried fruit, grated rinds and nuts into a large bowl and mix well. Whisk the egg with the orange and lemon juice, add the brandy and mix in, together with the ale. Mix well, then cover and leave for several hours or overnight. Next day mix again and spoon into a greased 1.5 litre (2½ pint) bowl. Cover with greased greaseproof paper and foil and secure well. Steam for 4 hours.

Store in a cool, dry place; steam for another 3 hours before serving.

SPICED PLUM CRUMBLE

This is just a spicy version of an old favourite that always seems to be popular.

Serves 6

700g (1 1/2 lb) plums
75–125g (3–4 oz) sugar

For the topping

225g (8 oz) plain wholewheat
  flour
1 teaspoon baking powder
1 teaspoon allspice

75g (3 oz) sugar
75g (3 oz) polyunsaturated
  margarine

Set the oven to 190°C (375°F), gas mark 5. Halve the plums and take out the stones. Put the plums into a shallow pie dish and sprinkle with the sugar. To make the topping, sift the flour, baking powder and allspice into a bowl, adding the bran left in the sieve too. Mix in the sugar and then blend in the margarine – it may be easiest to use a fork for this – until the mixture looks like fine breadcrumbs. Sprinkle this over the top of the plums in an even layer and press down lightly. Bake for 45 minutes.

Bread, Biscuits and Cakes

For this section I have chosen the breads, cakes and biscuits which are useful for serving with the other dishes in the book or for adding the finishing touch to the feast. The raspberry Victoria sponge, the chocolate gâteau with hazel nuts and the candied peel, ginger and almond cake all come into this last category.

Perhaps more down-to-earth, but still delicious, are the various crisp biscuits and the cheese, mustard and sesame scones, which can all be made fairly quickly. Also the fragrant herb bread, which, though more time-consuming to make, fills the kitchen with a wonderful fragrance of herbs as it bakes. This is delicious served warm with soups and cream cheese mixtures. The part-baked rolls are also useful because you can freeze them and then finish baking them when you want to serve hot rolls, fresh from the oven.

___

HERB BREAD

Served warm from the oven, fragrant herb bread is delicious with soup, especially the artichoke or cauliflower soup on pages 44 and 46. This bread takes just 2 hours to make from start to finish.

Makes one 450g (1 lb) loaf

6 tablespoons milk
6 tablespoons hot water
15g ($^1/_2$ oz) fresh yeast *or* 2 teaspoons dried yeast and $^1/_2$ teaspoon sugar
275g (10 oz) wholewheat flour
4 teaspoons sugar

1 teaspoon salt
25g (1 oz) soft butter *or* polyunsaturated margarine
1 small onion, peeled and finely grated
$^1/_2$ teaspoon dried oregano
$^1/_2$ teaspoon dried savory

Mix together the milk and water to make a lukewarm liquid. If you're using fresh yeast, crumble it into a small bowl and gradually blend in the milk and water with a spoon. For dried yeast, put the milk and water into a bowl then sprinkle in the yeast and sugar; stir once. Leave on one side for 10 minutes until the yeast has frothed up with a head, like a glass of beer.

Put the flour, sugar and salt, into a large bowl and rub in the butter or margarine, then mix in the onion and herbs. Make a well in the centre and pour in the yeast mixture. Mix together to form a soft dough which leaves the sides of the bowl clean. Turn the dough out onto a clean working surface and knead for 10 minutes, until the texture becomes smooth and pliable. Then put the dough back into the mixing bowl, cover the bowl with a piece of clingfilm and leave for 40–45 minutes, until doubled in size.

Set the oven to 230°C (450°F), gas mark 8. Take the dough out of the bowl and press it firmly all over with your knuckles to 'knock back' the dough and remove any large pockets of air. Knead for 2 minutes, then form the dough into a rectangle, roll it over so that the seam is underneath and drop it into a greased 450g (1 lb) loaf tin, pressing the corners down well into the tin so that the centre is nice and rounded. Cover with a damp cloth or a piece of clingfilm and leave in a warm place for 20–30 minutes to rise. Bake in the pre-heated oven for 10 minutes, then turn the oven setting down to 200°C (400°F), gas mark 6, and bake the bread for a further 25 minutes. Turn the loaf out on to a wire tray to cool. It's nicest served warm from the oven, cut into thick slices.

SOFT BREAD ROLLS

These wholewheat rolls turn out light and fluffy inside, and are easy to make. If you like them, you might like to make a bigger batch, using 25g (1 oz) fresh yeast or 1 tablespoon dried yeast and double the other ingredients given, to make 24 rolls. And you can make very good hot cross buns from this recipe by adding a teaspoonful of mixed spice and 125g (4 oz) dried fruit, then brushing the buns when they come out of the oven with a glaze made by melting 2 tablespoons of sugar in 1 tablespoon of milk.

Makes 12 rolls

25g (1 oz) fresh yeast *or* 1
    tablespoon dried yeast
1 teaspoon sugar
150ml (^{1}/4 pint) lukewarm milk
350g (12 oz) wholewheat flour

1 teaspoon salt
25g (1 oz) soft butter *or*
    vegetable margarine
1 egg, beaten

If you're using fresh yeast, crumble it into a small bowl and gradually blend in the milk with a spoon. For dried yeast, put the milk into a bowl, then stir in the sugar and sprinkle in the yeast; stir once. Leave on one side for 10 minutes until the yeast has frothed up with a head, like a glass of beer.

195

Put the flour and salt (and sugar, if you're using fresh yeast) into a large bowl and rub in the fat with your fingertips. Make a well in the centre and pour in the yeast mixture and add the beaten egg. Mix together to a soft dough. Turn the dough out onto a clean working surface and knead for 10 minutes, until the texture becomes smooth and pliable. Then put the dough back into the mixing bowl, cover the bowl with a piece of clingfilm and leave at room temperature for 1½ hours to rise.

Set the oven to 220°C (425°F), gas mark 7. Take the dough out of the bowl and press it firmly all over with your knuckles to 'knock back' and remove any large pockets of air. Knead for 2 minutes, then divide the dough into 24 pieces and form each into a smooth roll. Place the rolls about 2.5cm (1 in) apart on a greased baking sheet, cover with clingfilm or a clean cloth and leave in a warm place for 30 minutes to rise. Bake for 20 minutes, until the rolls are browned and sound hollow when you turn one over and tap it on the base with your knuckles.

FREEZER ROLLS

It's very convenient to be able to take a batch of partly-cooked rolls from the freezer, finish them off in the oven and serve them fresh and warm. You can do this if you bake them first at a low temperature, then freeze them and finish them off as usual when you need them. Follow the previous recipe, but bake the rolls at 150°C (300°F), gas mark 2, for 20 minutes, just to 'set' the rolls. Cool them completely, then pack in polythene bags and freeze. To use, let the rolls thaw out at room temperature for 45–60 minutes, then bake at 230°C (450°F), gas mark 8 for 10 minutes. They can be cooked while still frozen, if you're desperate, but may take a bit longer, about 15 minutes.

MELBA TOAST

You can make excellent melba toast from sliced wholewheat bread and it makes a lovely crunchy accompaniment to creamy dips and pâtés. It's delicious, and people always eat more than you think they will, so make plenty!

1 or 2 slices ready-sliced wholewheat bread for each person

Set the oven to 200°C (400°F), gas mark 6. Make the bread into toast in the usual way, then lay the piece of toast flat on a board and, using a sharp knife and a sawing motion, cut the bread in half horizontally. Place the toast halves, uncooked side-uppermost, on a baking sheet and bake for about 7–10 minutes, until they are crisp and brown all over, and curling up at the edges. Cool.

CHEESE, MUSTARD AND SESAME SCONES

These scones can be made from start to finish in 20–30 minutes and they are lovely for serving with soup to make it into more of a meal, or with a vegetable gratin or stew instead of potatoes. They are also nice to take on a picnic.

Makes about 12

225g (8 oz) plain wholewheat flour
4 teaspoons baking powder
1 teaspoon mustard powder
$1/2$ teaspoon sea salt
50g (2 oz) polyunsaturated margarine

150g (5 oz) cheese, finely grated
8–10 tablespoons buttermilk – this is best, but if you can't get it, milk also gives good results
sesame seeds

197

Set the oven to 220°C (425°F), gas mark 7. Sift the flour, baking powder, mustard and salt into a large bowl, adding the bran left in the sieve, too. Using your fingertips, rub the fat into the flour until the mixture looks like fine breadcrumbs. Lightly mix in 125g (4 oz) of the grated cheese, then enough of the buttermilk or milk to make a soft dough that leaves the sides of the bowl clean. Sprinkle a board with sesame seeds and turn the dough out onto them. Knead the dough briefly then roll it out in the sesame seeds to a thickness of about 2.5cm (1 in), pressing the sesame seeds into the dough and turning the dough over so that both sides get coated. Use a 5cm (2 in) cutter to cut the dough into rounds. Place the rounds on a floured baking sheet, sprinkle the rest of the cheese on top of the scones. Bake at the top of the pre-heated oven for about 12 minutes until the scones are risen and golden-brown. Cool on a wire rack.

BABY SCONES

The scones can be made from the same mixture cut out with a tiny round cutter measuring 1cm ($^1/_2$ in) across; or you can leave out the cheese and mustard and add 50g (2 oz) sugar instead, for a sweet version. They are a bit fiddly to make but are very suitable for a buffet or drinks party, split and topped with various sweet and savoury dips. Using a small cutter the quantities above should give about thirty scones and they will take about 10 minutes to cook.

WHOLEWHEAT CHEESE STRAWS

Cheese straws are always popular and useful for serving with drinks and dips.

Makes about 80

125g (4 oz) plain wholewheat flour

$1/2$ teaspoon baking powder

a good pinch of cayenne pepper

sea salt and freshly ground black pepper

75g (3 oz) butter *or* polyunsaturated margarine

75g (3 oz) Cheddar cheese, finely grated

Set the oven to 200°C (400°F), gas mark 6. Sift the flour with the baking powder, cayenne pepper and some salt and freshly ground black pepper, adding the bran left in the sieve, too. Using your fingertips, rub the fat into the flour until the mixture looks like fine breadcrumbs. Lightly mix in the grated cheese and press mixture together to make a soft but firm dough. Turn the dough out onto a lightly-floured board; knead briefly then roll out about 3mm ($1/8$ in) thick and cut into straws about 3mm ($1/8$ in) wide and 5cm (2 in) long. Put the straws on a floured baking sheet and bake in the pre-heated oven for about 7–10 minutes until they are crisp and golden-brown. Cool on a wire rack – they will get crisper as they cool.

CRUNCHY GINGER BISCUITS

Crunchy ginger biscuits are useful for serving with creamy puddings, for children's tea-parties or taking on picnics. These are generally popular and are quick and easy to make. If you find the texture of wholewheat flour rather heavy, don't put back the bran after you have sifted the flour, but use it to 'flour' the baking sheet. That way you will still be getting the balanced goodness of the whole flour, but with a lighter texture.

Makes about 30

125g (4 oz) plain wholewheat flour

1 teaspoon baking powder

1 teaspoon ground ginger

$1/2$ teaspoon bicarbonate of soda

125g (4 oz) porridge oats

125g (4 oz) polyunsaturated margarine

125g (4 oz) demerara sugar

1 rounded tablespoon golden syrup

Set the oven to 180°C (350°F), gas mark 4. Sift the flour, baking powder, ginger and bicarbonate of soda into a bowl, keeping the residue of bran from the sieve on one side for the moment; add the oats to the mixture. Put the margarine, sugar and golden syrup in a medium-sized, heavy-based saucepan and heat gently until melted. Remove from the heat and stir in the flour mixture. Grease a baking sheet with butter and sprinkle with the reserved bran from the sieve. Form teaspoons of the mixture into small balls, place well apart on the tray and flatten each with a fork. Bake for 15 minutes. Leave to cool on the tray for 5 minutes, then transfer to a wire rack to finish cooling.

SHORTBREAD HEARTS

These are just nice crisp biscuits which melt in your mouth and are useful for serving with creamy puddings or at tea time. Of course you don't have to make these heart-shaped; they are also good for children's parties with icing on them and a sprinkling of coloured sugar strands and in this case you'll probably be cutting them out in the shapes of teddy bears, engines, cars and so on!

Makes about 60 small hearts

175g (6 oz) plain 81 per cent
   wholewheat flour
50g (2 oz) caster sugar

175g (6 oz) butter *or*
   polyunsaturated margarine

Set the oven to 180°C (350°F), gas mark 4. Sift the flour into a bowl, keeping the residue of bran from the sieve on one side for the moment. Add the sugar, then blend in the butter or margarine with a fork until the mixture looks like fine breadcrumbs. Press mixture gently together to make a dough. Sprinkle a board with the bran from the sieve, turn the dough on to this and knead lightly, then roll out to a thickness of about 3mm (1/8 in) and stamp into hearts (or other shapes) with a pastry cutter. Put the shapes on a baking sheet and bake for 15–20 minutes. Leave to cool on the sheet for 5 minutes, then transfer to a wire rack to finish cooling.

THIN CRISP GINGER BISCUITS

This is really a variation of the shortbread hearts and made in exactly the same way except that you sift 1 teaspoonful of ground ginger with the flour and increase the amount of sugar to 75g (3 oz).

VANILLA DROPS

These are melt-in-the-mouth biscuits which are piped on to a baking sheet.

Makes 12

60g (2¹/₂ oz) 81 per cent
   wholewheat flour
25g (1 oz) cornflour
25g (1 oz) caster sugar

75g (3 oz) polyunsaturated
   margarine
1 teaspoon vanilla essence
icing sugar to dredge

Set the oven to 180°C (350°F), gas mark 4. Sift the flour and cornflour into a bowl, then add all the remaining ingredients and beat together to make a soft, light mixture. Spoon this mixture into a piping bag fitted with a large star nozzle, and pipe stars on to a lightly-greased baking sheet. Bake for about 20 minutes, until set and golden brown. Leave to cool on the tray for 5 minutes, then transfer to a wire rack to finish cooling.

RASPBERRY VICTORIA SPONGE

A light sandwich cake filled with fresh or frozen raspberries and whipped cream and dredged with icing sugar, this is lovely for a special tea in summer. If you want to cut down on fat, you can replace the cream with curd cheese, whisked with a little milk until light and creamy; or use half cream and half *fromage blanc*.

Makes one 20cm (8 in) cake

125g (4 oz) 81 per cent self-raising wholewheat flour	125g (4 oz) caster sugar
1 teaspoon baking powder	125g (4 oz) polyunsaturated margarine
2 eggs	a few drops of milk

For the filling

150ml ($^1/_4$ pint) whipping cream, whipped	icing sugar
125–175g (4–6 oz) fresh *or* frozen raspberries, thawed	

Set the oven to 180°C (350°F), gas mark 4. Line two 20cm (8 in) sandwich tins with circles of greaseproof paper and brush with oil. Sift the flour and baking powder into a bowl, then put in all the remaining cake ingredients and beat by hand or electricity for 2–3 minutes, until light and creamy. Add up to 1 tablespoonful of milk, a little at a time, if necessary to make the mixture soft enough to drop easily when you shake the spoon. Divide the mixture between the two tins and smooth the tops. Bake for 20 minutes, until the cakes are well risen and spring back when pressed lightly with a fingertip. Turn the cakes out onto a wire rack to cool, then strip off the paper. Spread one of the cakes with half the cream and put the raspberries on top; sprinkle with a little icing sugar, then spread with the rest of the cream and place the other cake on top. Dredge with icing sugar. Serve as soon as possible.

CHOCOLATE GÂTEAU
WITH HAZEL NUTS

This is a luscious cake – rich and very fattening, but highly suitable for a special occasion.

Makes one 20cm (8 in) cake

175g (6 oz) 81 per cent
  self-raising wholewheat flour
1 rounded tablespoon cocoa
  powder
1¹/2 teaspoons baking powder

3 eggs
175g (6 oz) caster sugar
175g (6 oz) polyunsaturated
  margarine
1–2 tablespoons milk

For the filling and topping

1 egg
150ml (¹/4 pint) milk
75g (3 oz) sugar
125g (4 oz) plain chocolate
225g (8 oz) unsalted butter *or*
  unsalted polyunsaturated
  margarine

50g (2 oz) chopped roasted hazel
  nuts – these can be bought in a
  packet, or you can make your
  own, see page 36
a few whole hazel nuts,
  preferably roasted and with
  the skins rubbed off

Set the oven to 180°C (350°F), gas mark 4. Line two 20cm (8 in) sandwich tins with greaseproof paper and brush with oil. Sift the flour, cocoa and baking powder into a bowl, then put in all the remaining cake ingredients and beat by hand or electricity for 2–3 minutes, until light and creamy. Add up to 2 tablespoonfuls of milk, a little at a time, if necessary to make the mixture soft enough to drop easily when you shake the spoon. Divide the mixture between the tins and smooth the tops. Bake for 30 minutes, until the cakes are well risen and spring back when pressed lightly with a fingertip. Turn the cakes out onto a wire rack to cool, then strip off the paper.

Meanwhile make the butter icing for the filling and topping. Put the egg, milk and sugar into a small saucepan and whisk together until smooth. Heat gently, stirring all the time, until just beginning to thicken. Remove from the heat. Break up the chocolate and add this to the custard mixture: the heat of the custard will melt it. Stir occasionally, then leave on one side until cool. Beat the butter or margarine until light and fluffy, then gradually beat in the cold chocolate custard mixture.

Put 3 rounded tablespoons of the butter icing into a piping bag fitted with a large star nozzle; leave on one side for the moment. Split each of the cakes in half, so that you will have four layers. Sandwich the cakes together with some of the butter icing. Spread the sides of the cake with butter icing and coat with nuts. Cover the top of the cake with more icing, then with the reserved icing pipe a whirl of icing in the centre and more round the edge. Decorate with a few whole hazel nuts.

CANDIED PEEL, GINGER AND ALMOND CAKE

This cake is rather an indulgence on my part because I have included three of my favourite cake ingredients: candied peel, almonds and crystallized ginger! It makes a pleasant change from the usual Dundee cake.

Makes one 20cm (8 in) cake

225g (8 oz) plain wholewheat flour
1 heaped teaspoon baking powder
175g (6 oz) polyunsaturated margarine
175g (6 oz) soft brown sugar
3 eggs, beaten
225g (8 oz) candied peel, quite finely chopped

225g (8 oz) crystallized ginger, roughly chopped
125g (4 oz) angelica, chopped
grated rind of 1 lemon
125g (4 oz) ground almonds
50g (2 oz) flaked almonds
3–4 tablespoons milk
a little clear honey, to glaze

Set the oven to 180°C (350°F), gas mark 4. Line a 20cm (8 in) round tin with greased greaseproof paper. Sift the flour with the baking powder and mix in the bran which is left in the sieve. Cream the margarine and sugar until light and fluffy, then slowly add the beaten eggs, one at a time, beating all the time and adding a little flour if the mixture starts to curdle. Fold in the flour and all the other ingredients, adding enough milk to make a soft consistency which drops easily from the spoon. Put the mixture into the tin and bake for 2 hours, until a warmed skewer inserted into the centre of the cake comes out clean. Cool for 5 minutes in the tin, then turn out onto a wire rack to finish cooling. Strip off the paper when the cake is cold, then warm a little honey and brush this all over the cake to make it look shiny and appetizing.

Index

Index

A

Index

D

Dão 28
Dairy produce
  note on 35-6
  protein in 32-4
Deep dish
  mushroom pie 140-1
  stripy vegetable pie 141-3
Dessert wine 31
Dhal sauce, spiced vegetables
  with 123-4
Dijon mustard 39
Dinner
  Christmas 13-15
  parties 15-18
Dip(s) 59-68
  Cheddar cheese and red wine
    61
  creamy butter bean, with
    sesame toast 60-1
  soured cream and herb, with
    crudités 63
Dressings, salad 158-67
Drinks parties, buffets and
  receptions 25-6
Drops, vanilla 201

E

Egg(s)
  and cheese dishes: 150-7
  hardboiled, bean and black
    olive pâté with 59-60
  sauce, fennel with 103
  vegetarian Scotch 153

F

Fats, note on 37
Fennel 39
  apple and cucumber salad 85
  with egg sauce 103
Festive sprouts 97-8
Fino sherry 28
First courses 51-77
  wines for 28-9
Flaky
  mushroom roll 143-4
  pastry, quick 143-4
Flan
  almond and chocolate 184-5
  asparagus 135-7
  aubergine, red pepper and
    cheese 137-8
  cauliflower, Stilton and
    walnut 139-40
  jewelled fruit 189-90
Flavouring ingredients, note on
  39
Flour, note on 37-8
Fondue, cheese 150-1
Frascati 28
Freezer bread rolls 196
Freezing pulses 37
Fresh mangoes 177
Fromage blanc, note on 35
Fruit
  flan, jewelled 189-90
  salad, special 176-7
  and vegetable dishes (first
    courses) 52-8
Fruity puddings: 176-83

213

Index

Index